Planktonia

Planktonia

*The Nightly Migration of
the Ocean's Smallest Creatures*

ERICH HOYT

FIREFLY BOOKS

A Firefly Book

Published by Firefly Books Ltd. 2022

First printing

Library of Congress Control Number: 2022932815

Library and Archives Canada Cataloguing in Publication
Title: Planktonia : the nightly migration of the ocean's
   smallest creatures / Erich Hoyt.
Names: Hoyt, Erich, author.
Description: Includes index.
Identifiers: Canadiana 20220175225 | ISBN 9780228103837 (hardcover)
Subjects: LCSH: Marine plankton—Vertical distribution. |
   LCSH: Marine plankton.
Classification: LCC QH91.8.P5 H69 2022 | DDC 578.77/6—dc23

Published in the United States by
Firefly Books (U.S.) Inc.
P.O. Box 1338, Ellicott Station
Buffalo, New York 14205

Published in Canada by
Firefly Books Ltd.
50 Staples Avenue, Unit 1
Richmond Hill, Ontario L4B 0A7

Cover and interior design: Stacey Cho
Front cover: juvenile deep water pelagic octopus (*Vitreledonella richardi*), Cape
   Verde, Atlantic Ocean. Photograph by Solvin Zankl (Nature Public Library).
Back cover, top: sea angel (*Clione limacina*). Photograph by Alexander Semenov.
Back cover, bottom: paper nautilus and tunicate (*Argonauta hians* and Genus
   Pyrosoma). Photograph by Magnus Lundgren (Nature Public Library).
Back cover, flap: porcupinefish (Genus *Diodon*). Photograph by Linda Ianniello.

Printed in China

We acknowledge the financial support of the Government of Canada.

To Sarah, with all my love

The word "planktonia,"
borrowed from the Finnish language,
conjures up the vast universe of tiny plankton and predators
in all their brilliant colors, clever designs,
and unnerving beauty.

Author's Note

When people hear the word "migration," they often think of humpback whales, Arctic caribou, albatrosses, leatherback sea turtles, animals that move from a feeding area to a breeding area and back each year. But the greatest migration on Earth happens twice every night. The movement is largely vertical and largely performed by plankton, organisms that drift in the ocean's currents, and micronekton, the small animals that can actively swim against those currents, accompanied by followers and hangers-on, including predatory fishes, squid, octopus and other species, that have acquired a taste for plankton. The migration starts deep in the waters of the ocean every evening at sunset. The nighttime migration is composed of miniature creatures of intricate design, a riot of color, near-transparency or iridescence and flashing lights. As they move, the zooplankton — the animals — nibble on phytoplankton — the tiny plants of the plankton — and other tasty morsels in the water and, eventually, some of them on each other. The feeding ends just before dawn when the plankton retreat to the depths of the ocean to hide during the day until, once again, the next evening, they migrate back up the water column.

Most of the creatures in this book are larval planktonic marvels, tiny and either beautiful or terribly strange depending on your perspective. There are adult creatures in the ocean at night, too, that come to feast under the cover of darkness. On a cloudless, full-moon night, they might stay a little deeper or wait longer to begin their ascent, but they soon move up and begin to feed. At the same time, these planktonic creatures must try to avoid being eaten themselves. Night is safer from the jaws of certain hungry creatures with big eyes and much bigger appetites. Still, there are the specialist predators of the night — squid jetting around this way and that, jellyfish tentacles dangling everywhere in wait for the unwary, and even the all-engulfing mouth of a basking shark or a giant blue whale.

But when human blackwater divers arrive, everything changes. Suddenly, the blackness vanishes and everything becomes almost bright as daylight when strong spotlights are switched on. Some plankton immediately descend, leaving the area. But others either remain and just hover, mesmerized by the light or perhaps too hungry to flee. They may continue feeding because they sense it couldn't be daytime yet; it couldn't be time to descend into the depths.

Amidst the dazzle and faint hum of the lights, a camera lens moves in and out, approaching within a hand's width of fingernail-size figures, fluttering in the current. One by one, each planktonic creature, each plankter (to use the singular form), has its moment in the spotlight, captured on video or still image, some plankton opening their mouths, others waving tentacles in hopes of catching food. Here, both plankton and diver drift in the current, swept up in the drama of life in the ocean.

This book is mainly about the nightlife of plankton and the photographers and researchers who are uncovering planktonic lives. There will also be cameos for some of the parents of these plankton and a few of the plankton predators, big and small. All of them are inhabitants of the night.

This book would not have been possible without the knowledge, passion and kindness of those researchers and photographers, who themselves have become creatures of the night, undertaking their own vertical migrations in the opposite direction — descending into the water after nightfall and coming up and out from their last dive in the middle of the night, sometimes close to daybreak. All in the service of exploring, photographing and learning more about this wondrous nighttime world.

My heartfelt thanks go to Alexander Semenov, Jeffrey Milisen, Linda Ianniello, Susan Mears, Mike Bartick and Ryo Minemizu with Tatsuo Ito for photographs as well as extensive interviews and checking text. Rachelle Morris from Nature Picture Library gave helpful information from photographers Magnus Lundgren, Alex Mustard and Doug Perrine. Ichthyologists Bruce C. Mundy, G. David Johnson and Ai Nonaka gave generously of their time to correct and comment on the text, and Alexander Semenov caught a few more errors. I can't thank them enough. I'm grateful to my editor Michael Worek, publisher Lionel Koffler and designer Stacey Cho for their contributions in making this book.

— Erich Hoyt
Bridport, Dorset, England
March 2022

Contents

CHAPTER 1
Introducing a Cast of Trillions

In 1817, French zoologist Georges Cuvier was the first to report the nightly vertical migration of plankton after witnessing it in a lake. In the late 1800s, Austrian geologist Theodor Fuchs took net samples at various depths of the open ocean to show that planktonic crustaceans were moving from deep to surface waters as night came on. But no one realized how prevalent vertical oceanic migrations were. During World War II, echo sounders on German U-boats in the North Atlantic found that the bottom of the ocean seemed to be moving up every night! After the war, scientists comparing the mass of plankton and micronekton, such as lanternfishes, that they collected at different depths at night and in the day realized that this was a biological phenomenon happening all over the ocean from polar to tropical waters. The global vertical migration of plankton and micronekton was so massive it was read by the echo sounders as the bottom of the ocean.

This book describes the tiny ocean plankton that rise to the surface waters every evening to feed under the cover of night. As dawn breaks, the plankton move back down to their daytime home, a thousand or more feet (over 300 m) below the surface, some all the way to the bottom, only to return again in the evening. In terms of numbers, the many trillions of plankton that move up and down are far more numerous than the seabirds, marine turtles, sharks, seals and whales that undertake long oceanic or airborne journeys. They're even more numerous than the twice-a-day "migration" of hundreds of millions of human commuters around the world.

Not all plankton undertake vertical migrations. Some move horizontally, carried by local currents or great rivers of life like the Gulf Stream. Other plankton near the poles have much slower migrations, remaining in surface waters in the warmer months and descending to the depths as the surface water turns cold and starts to freeze. But nightly vertical migration is by far the most common.

Plankton mainly float about in the sea; that's the definition of plankton. Nekton includes most mature and juvenile fishes, squid and all the marine mammals and sea turtles, which are like Olympic athletes in water sports compared to plankton. The division between plankton and nekton is not sharp. Some animals will act like both. Some change from plankton when small to nekton as they grow, including most fishes and cephalopods. Others appear to act as both, depending on their behavior, such as large jellyfish and salps which often drift by but are also capable of strong swimming.

Swimming up and down the water column must be a heroic feat. To move upward, some plankton wave their arms like dancers or flap their tails; some use a kind of breaststroke with both limbs; others lurch ahead, often with one limb providing the thrust. It's amazing how fast you can move if you're hungry or trying to avoid being someone else's midnight feast. Still, even the plankton capable of basic swimming are no match for oceanic currents and tides.

Marine scientist Thomas Kiørboe and his colleagues studied these movements across a wide range of planktonic species and suggested that plankton that were feeding thrashed the water with abandon, but if they were just swimming to get to a feeding area, they made subtle swimming motions with their limbs so as not to disturb the water and alert predators. Kiørboe calculated that zooplankton must process water equivalent to up to one million times their own body volume to get enough to eat.

Plankton include many shallow, midwater and deep-sea species of fishes and invertebrates. Besides the many kinds of larval and juvenile fishes, the planktonic invertebrates include crustaceans (crabs, lobsters, crayfish, shrimps, prawns, krill), mollusks (squids, octopus, snails, slugs), cnidarians (corals, hydrozoans, jellyfish, siphonophores, as well as larvae of sea anemones, sea pens, sea whips,

sea fans), ctenophores (comb jellies) and tunicates (salps, doliolids, pyrosomes and larval sea squirts). In the words of researchers, plankton have huge taxonomic diversity with many thousands of undiscovered species.

Some species of aquatic life are plankton only as larvae, growing up, for example, to be barnacles and crabs on the seabed or fishes that become strong swimmers. They're called merozooplankton. Others, such as some jellyfish, salps and more, remain plankton all their lives. They're the holozooplankton.

And, as divers with macro lenses and a lot of patience are demonstrating and this book reveals, plankton are not drab; they come in all colors, shapes and forms. They come with feathery fins, transparent torsos and bejeweled eyes. Photographed with macro lenses, they come alive. Plankton are extraordinarily beautiful for the most part, but some may appear menacing or even frightening.

Plankton can be plants (phytoplankton) or animals (zooplankton). The source of the ocean's productivity lies in the phytoplankton, which are produced by energy from the sun. Because this activity happens near the ocean surface, it attracts zooplankton to migrate into upper waters. Phytoplankton are both the fundamental food for zooplankton and a vast carbon storage bank that helps in the fight against climate change. Keeping the ocean healthy starts with keeping phytoplankton healthy. All the fishes, the fishing industry and those who eat fish depend upon the zooplankton that eat phytoplankton. Even whales depend on the zooplankton eating phytoplankton. Thus, phytoplankton are so important that a substantial portion of life on Earth and the planet itself depend on them for survival.

Dinoflagellates are phytoplankton that are sometimes dangerous to humans, whales and other creatures. When dinoflagellate algae take advantage of warm or polluted waters, exploding to huge population levels, the waters can turn red from the dinoflagellates' red plastids, the subcellular structures or organelles containing one type of photosynthetic pigment. As the toxins from this "red tide" move through the food chain, they become concentrated enough to kill. Certain jellyfish and siphonophores can sometimes fatally wound humans with their stinging nematocysts — for example, the Portuguese man o' war and some species of box jellyfish — but much more dangerous are the dinoflagellates and other single-celled phytoplankton, such as algae and cyanobacteria, when they are being fed by an overabundance of nutrients from agricultural chemicals and sewage runoff into rivers and the ocean. The exponential growth of phytoplankton leads to algal blooms. When they multiply, they consume massive amounts of oxygen. Soon after, they die and as they decompose, bacteria jump in to consume most of the remaining oxygen. This kills any other living organisms in the area and creates a dead zone in the ocean. These dead zones number in the hundreds and extend over thousands of square miles of mostly coastal or inland sea areas. Well-known dead zones are the northern Gulf of Mexico and parts of the Baltic Sea, but they exist in every ocean. Some of them are temporary or seasonal, but many are permanent.

It's in the zooplankton that plankton really show their extraordinary diversity of species. Zooplankton also have a large size range from microns to centimeters and more, as shown in the table on the opposite page. They can be so tiny that hundreds of them fit on the head of a pin. Femtoplankton is the smallest — comprising the marine viruses — ranging up to the megaplankton, which includes many jellyfish, krill, ctenophores, the larger salps and tunicates, and siphonophores. To be megaplankton in good standing, the animal needs to be at least 7 ⅞ inches (20 cm) long. These also include the hydrozoans, such as the Portuguese man o' war (*Physalia physalis*) and the by-the-wind sailor (*Velella velella*), which move at the mercy of the currents. Because they float largely on the surface, they are sometimes referred to as neuston, a category of the plankton found only in that habitat. But they do drift, too.

The largest, or longest, megaplankton are the lion's mane jellyfish (*Cyanea capillata*), whose dome diameter is up to 7 ½ feet (2.3 m) with tentacles measuring up to 123 feet (37.5 m), and the colonial siphonophore *Apolemia* with estimated measurements up to 390 feet (119 m). The lion's mane is a single creature that is well known to measure longer than even the record 100 foot (30.5 m) blue whale. The siphonophore *Apolemia*, however, is actually a massive colony of connected bodies. The record size *Apolemia* was encountered in a spiral feeding pose during a 2020 expedition in the Indian Ocean west of Australia. Exact measurements could not be undertaken, but it was estimated to be more than three times longer than the record size of the lion's mane.

Large, heavy megaplankton may also include the bumphead ocean sunfish (*Mola alexandrini*), which measures up to 10 feet 10 inches long (3.3 m) and weighs up to 3.3 tons (3,000 kg), and other *Mola* species. *Mola* are fishes that typically float with the currents, using their dorsal and pectoral fins mainly to steer. Some researchers and divers say that sunfishes are not plankton, that they can move fast if they have to, and may even undertake migrations to higher latitudes during spring and summer months following their own plankton prey.

Whales eat mostly the middle to large varieties of plankton — the copepods and krill that inhabit vast parts

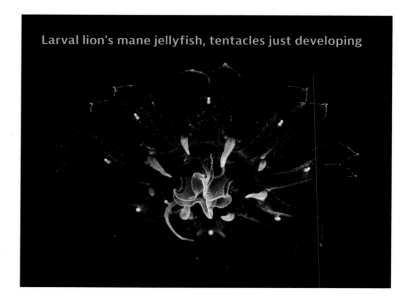

Larval lion's mane jellyfish, tentacles just developing

Plankton, by size

Type of zooplankton	Size range	Size comparison	Description
Femtoplankton	0.02–0.2 µm (micron) (From 0.0000007874 to 0.000007874 of an inch)	< 1/40th the size of a red blood cell	Marine viruses
Picoplankton	0.2–2 µm (From 0.000007874 to 0.00007874 of an inch)	< ¼ the size of a red blood cell	Mainly bacteria
Nanoplankton	2–20 µm (From 0.00007874 to 0.0007874 of an inch)	From ¼ the size of a red blood cell to more than 2x the size	Unicellular zooplankton that feed on phytoplankton, amoebas, ciliates
Microplankton	20–200 µm (from 0.0007874 to 0.007874 of an inch))	From 2x the size of a red blood cell to 2x the thickness of a human hair	Copepods, phytoplankton, multicellular zooplankton (metazoans)
Mesoplankton	0.2 to 20 mm (from 0.008 to ¾ of an inch)	From 2x the thickness of a human hair to a large ant	Most of the copepods, hydrozoans, some siphonophores, some tunicates, small fish larvae, small ctenophores
Macroplankton	2 to 20 cm (¾ inch to 7 ⅞ inches)	A large ant to a small newborn puppy	More copepods, amphipods, arrow worms, tunicates, salps, large ctenophores, large fish larvae
Megaplankton	> 20 cm (7 ⅞ inches)	A small newborn puppy to an Irish wolfhound	Many jellyfish, ctenophores, larger salps and tunicates, cephalopods, amphipods, krill, sunfish

Note: 1 micron (µm) = 1/1000th mm = 0.000039 of an inch; 1 mm = 1/100th cm = 1/25th of an inch; 1 cm = ⅜ of an inch

of the ocean, particularly in colder waters. Traditionally, plankton have been collected at sea by fine-meshed conical nets that funnel the plankton into a small bottle, but this process often damages their fragile bodies. Some of them have mangled fins and other appendages, many are contorted or broken apart and others look more like mush than the beautiful creatures displayed in this book.

Over the past decade, as macrophotography combined with diving in the open sea at night grew in popularity, divers began sending their photographs to scientists and asking them to identify the species they'd photographed. In some cases, at first, the scientists had only general ideas of what they were looking at. For the fishes, drawing on years of plankton research from net samples, and studying the body shapes, fin placements, numbers of fin elements and muscle segments, the scientists could usually identify family and often genus, but sometimes not the species. The fin shapes and other fragile parts of the planktonic larvae looked very different than the eventual adult forms. In cases like those, identifications have depended on the ability of the diver to collect an individual so that scientists could match the DNA of the larval plankter to the adult. With the collection of specimens for genetic analysis, a whole new field has started to open. The photographers in this book — some of them part-time scientists, some working with scientists, some citizen scientists — aim to contribute to that literature, working to identify unknown species and capture their behavior with a camera.

Welcome to the world of plankton: *planktonia*.

Diverse zooplankton species are attracted by a diver's light at night. Most of the species shown here are crustaceans less than 3/8 inch (1 cm) in length. Of special note are decapod larvae, including mantis shrimps and adult copepods. During the day, most of these species avoid predators by staying at 100 to 200 foot (30 to 60 m) depths or more, migrating to shallower depths at night to feed. If they are guided by moonlight, as scientists theorize, that may explain why some are attracted to light sources underwater at night, including divers' lights.

The great vertical migration of plankton occurs every night across the global ocean. Here, in the surface waters of the Philippine Sea off Palau, millions of zooplankton enjoy the abundance of nutrients available in phyto-plankton, as they try to eat and avoid being eaten.

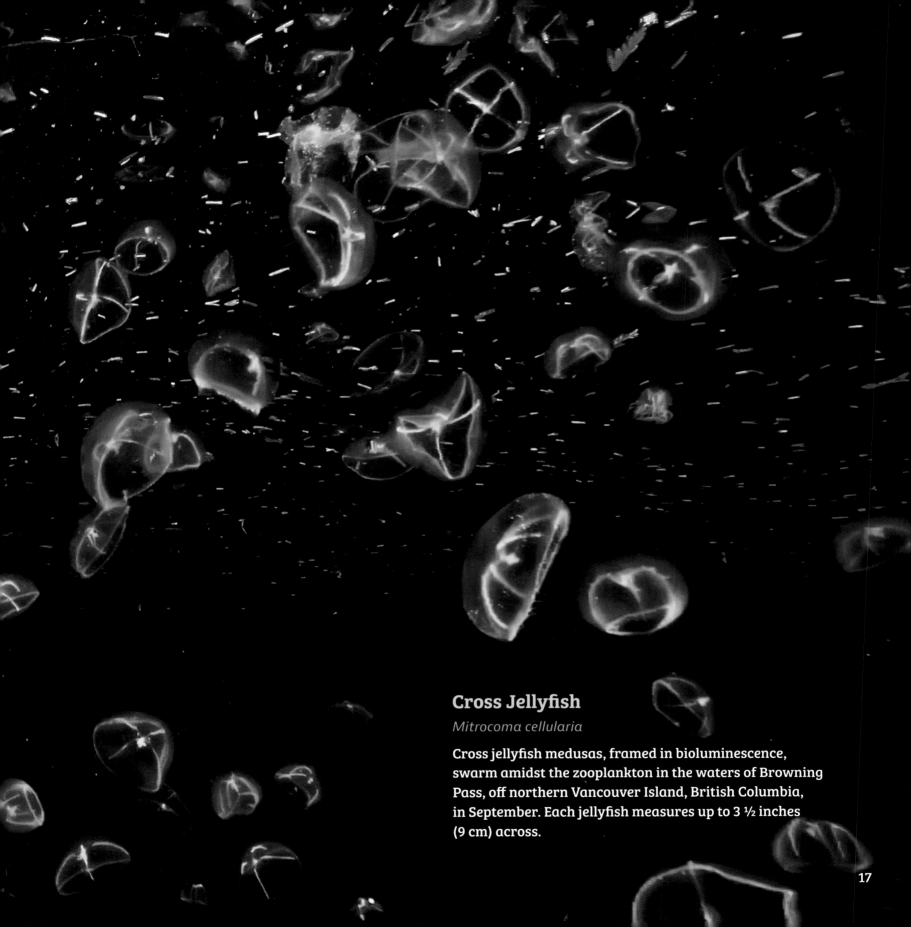

Cross Jellyfish

Mitrocoma cellularia

Cross jellyfish medusas, framed in bioluminescence, swarm amidst the zooplankton in the waters of Browning Pass, off northern Vancouver Island, British Columbia, in September. Each jellyfish measures up to 3 ½ inches (9 cm) across.

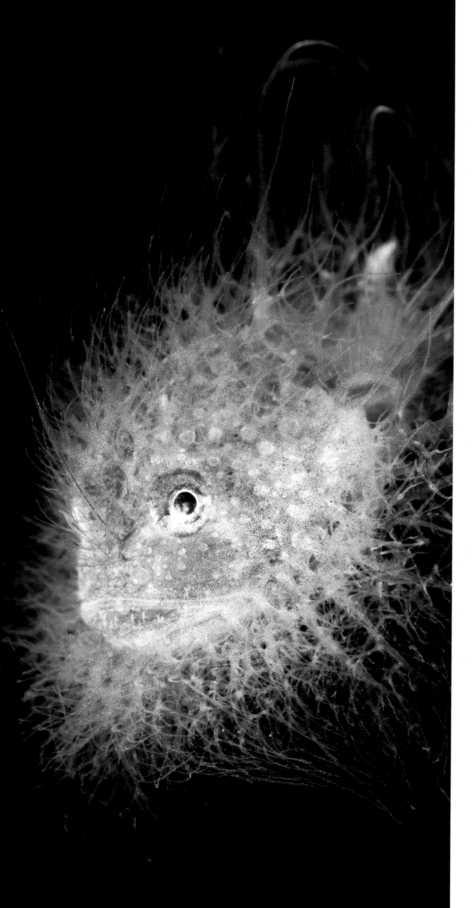

CHAPTER 2
Hawai'i: From Bluewater to Blackwater

Bluewater diving far from shore during daylight hours started in the early 1960s in places like the Mediterranean Sea and southern California. Bluewater divers, tethered to ropes attached to a central line suspended from a boat or buoy, could observe the natural environment far from the coastline or reefs where diving had always been done. The adventurers were mostly photographers and a few scientists trying to get an idea of what was going on with plankton and other species above the deep waters of the open ocean. One pioneer was ecologist-evolutionary biologist William Hamner, from the University of California, Los Angeles (UCLA), who developed bluewater diving and drifting techniques that are still used today.

After the Mediterranean and California, one of the favorite spots for early bluewater diving was off the Big Island of Hawai'i, built up from the ocean floor by volcanoes with steep drop-offs. The depths offshore are 3,300 feet (1,000 m) ranging up to 16,500 feet (5,000 m). Imagine being in the open ocean with no land, no bottom, no reference point in sight. That's what photographer Christopher Newbert wanted to experience in the early 1980s, as he went diving in the deep waters off Kona, Hawai'i. Then he decided to try something new — diving in open water at night. Divers had gone night diving before, but never in the boundless black of the open ocean. Blackwater diving was born.

"It was pretty wild," says Jeff Milisen, marine biologist and photographer who leads blackwater diving tours off

« **The hairy goosefish showing its jellyfish-like tentacles**

Kona. "Newbert was diving alone, grabbing hold of a line, jumping out of his own boat far from shore, descending as deep as 150 feet (46 m). He actually lost his boat a couple times. Fishermen reported picking him up the next morning. They would go and find his boat and then you'd hear that he'd done it again." These days, safety precautions for night diving are firmly in place.

"Newbert was the first one to publish photos and say 'hey guys, there's some fun stuff down here,'" adds Jeff. In 1984, more than 20 of Newbert's night photos were published in his landmark book, *Within a Rainbowed Sea*, providing some of the first glimpses of the nocturnal activities of pelagic Hawaiian marine life. Way ahead of its time, the book became a must read for anyone interested in the

delicate patterns and gaudy colors of ocean found not only in the day but also in the utter blackness of the night sea.

For the past six years, Jeff has been taking advantage of every sleepless night to go diving in the deep waters off Oahu and, more recently, off the west side of the big island from the Kona coast. His photograph of a cookie-cutter shark was his first publication, and he was soon hooked. His current day job in aquaculture technology fits neatly with the night dives for Kona Honu Divers. Jeff admits, "I've never really wanted to spend time just looking through microscopes. Really, I was much more interested in seeing and interacting with animals. And taking photographs of them."

Jeff understands how special Hawai'i is, being in the middle of the vast Pacific Ocean with a high percentage

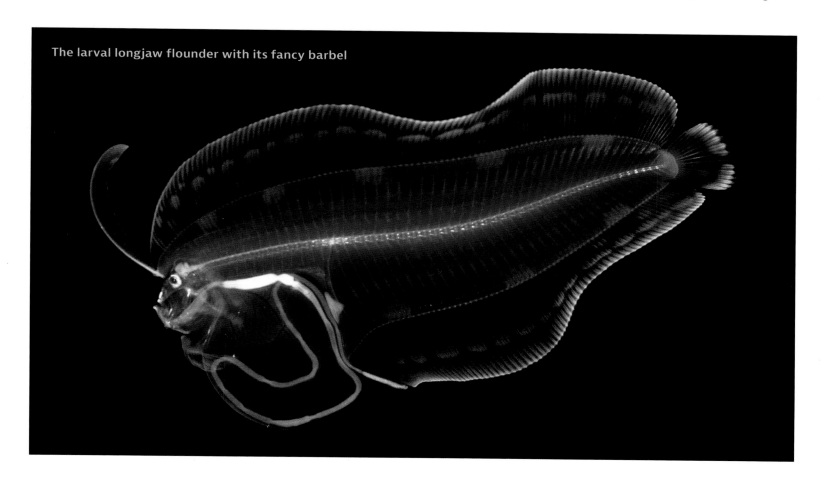

The larval longjaw flounder with its fancy barbel

of endemic species. "A few pioneer organisms have made the transoceanic journey which means that a lot of ocean animals did not. But the few that made it here had an empty slate of niches into which they could evolve rapidly. So, while we are missing some species like giant tridacna clams, groupers and cuttlefish, about 30% of the reef fishes and 30% of the mollusks here are unique. We do get big stuff here, swordfish, and huge shoals of squid that come in, including a bobtail squid that's only found here. But how this translates into what we see in blackwater — let's say it happens in ways we won't fully understand until we've done a lot more diving."

Jeff's dedication has led to the recently published *A Field Guide to Blackwater Diving in Hawai'i*. A labor of love, the guide reveals what's happening in Hawai'i's offshore waters. It includes the first photograph of the hairy goosefish (*Lophiodes fimbriatus*) to be seen in Hawaiian waters and larvae of some of the flounder species unique to the Hawaiian-Emperor Sea Mount chain.

Every blackwater dive leads to more questions and, these days, sending photographs to scientists. In 2016, diver-photographer Mike Bartick started the "Blackwater Photo Group" on Facebook, which has become a place for divers to post pictures for fellow divers and scientists to speculate on and confirm identifications. Two of the most helpful for identifications have been fish scientist (ichthyologist) Bruce C. Mundy, who worked for NOAA Fisheries in Hawai'i for 33 years, and G. David Johnson, a Curator of Fishes from the Smithsonian at the National Museum, Washington, DC. Most of what was known about planktonic larvae came through museums, where specimens have been fixed in formalin, stored in ethanol or an equivalent, after being collected in nets. These methods remove skin pigmentation, and the delicate larval fish fins are sometimes mangled.

Ichthyologists have known for some time that the evolution of the larval forms followed paths separate from the evolution of the adults. The larvae evolve in response to survival in the planktonic realm of the open ocean and the associated vertical migrations; the adults of most species might settle into different habitats ranging from the deep-sea bottom to shallow water reefs. What then would be the value of having elaborate feathery fins? As larvae, these modified fins make them look larger and perhaps more like a dangerous, stinging jellyfish (siphonophore) than an edible morsel. Evolution by natural selection plays a role in the presence of these elaborate productions, though ichthyologists are still trying to figure out the precise purposes of the various ornaments in the larval stages. By the time the mature flounder settles to the seabed, the flamboyant fins are gone. The strategy for survival as an adult becomes camouflage (changing color rapidly to match the bottom), along with two eyes on one side of its head, and burying itself partly in the sand.

Recently, Jeff and his diving partner and wife, Sarah Matye, began photographing more and more of the tiny larvae and occasionally taking video of them. As part of a collaborative study, they then collected individual

A venus girdle forming a defensive spiral

specimens for DNA analysis so that more definitive identifications could be made and connections could be forged between larvae and adults. Capturing a single tiny individual is a slow process to avoid contamination and damage. Once collected, each individual was carefully catalogued and made ready for shipment to the lab for DNA analysis by David Johnson, Ai Nonaka and others at the Smithsonian, where it would be placed in a permanent collection for further research.

On their blackwater dives off Kona, Hawai'i, Jeff and Sarah collected a total of 76 larval fish specimens for the analysis, each preserved in alcohol as a specimen, along with a tissue sample for genomic DNA extraction. This so-called DNA barcoding is a method that facilitates species identification. From the 76 specimens, 44 were identified to species or genus with a greater than 99% match, though nine were less than 99%. Thirteen could only be identified to family, one only to class. Two had no match in the database, indicating problems that need more research. Seven had a tissue sample that couldn't be analyzed due to various technical problems.

Three eel larvae in the study were the first to be identified to their species. One larval fish was the first of its genus to be identified.

They also captured unknown behavior, such as the habit of fish larvae to go jelly riding, attaching themselves to gelatinous organisms, which is thought to provide protection — like travelling with a bodyguard or riding in a tank. Some carried tiny jellyfish to sting those that dared bother them.

In March 2021, Jeff Milisen, along with Dave Johnson and Ai Nonaka from the Smithsonian and Bruce C. Mundy from Ocean Research Explorations, summarized their work in the paper "Blackwater Diving: An Exciting Window into the Planktonic Arena and Its Potential to Enhance the Quality of Larval Fish Collections." Following publication, *New York Times* journalist Erik Olsen contacted Jeff and his co-authors to interview them, as well as various

Box jellyfish, stinging nematocysts on its tentacles, at the ready

blackwater photography enthusiasts. The photos were splashed in vivid color across several pages. The story echoed the conclusions of the scientific paper — that scientist as well as non-scientist divers and photographers could make substantial contributions to the study of larvae if they not only photograph it but also, given the appropriate permits, if they collect some specimens for science. It was a call to action to go blackwater diving to advance our understanding of biodiversity in the ocean.

Leaf Scorpionfish Larva
Taenianotus triacanthus

As adults, leaf scorpionfish settle on coral reefs and try hard to blend in with their surroundings. They sometimes even sport algae or hydroids and have protrusions around the blotchy mouth that add to their camouflage strategy. Yet, as larvae, their fins are all show. This larval individual, 1 inch long (2.5 cm), flashes its handsome wings, coming right to the surface to feed at night. The common name "leaf" comes from the adult scorpionfish's ability to assume the appearance of a dead leaf on the bottom, even making undulating movements to resemble an inert drifting object. It does this to hunt, allowing unsuspecting small crustacean or larval prey to approach close before it opens its mouth and sucks in the food.

Diamond Squid

Thysanoteuthis rhombus

This just-hatched paralarval squid is about ⅜ inch long (1 cm). In only six to eight months, it will grow to more than 3 ¼ feet (1 m) in length. As it approaches maturity, this slow-moving squid will establish a life-long bond with its mate. As adults, the couple will be docile as squids go, finding their food among the more inactive fish. Diamond squids spend their days between 1,300 to nearly 2,000 feet (400–600 m) below the surface, ascending every night to feed in near-surface waters. The female produces up to 140,000 eggs during her life. Diamond squids have a maximum lifespan of one year. Although diamond squids live well offshore, lifeguards around Hawai'i have found pairs of them swimming inshore where they likely die together.

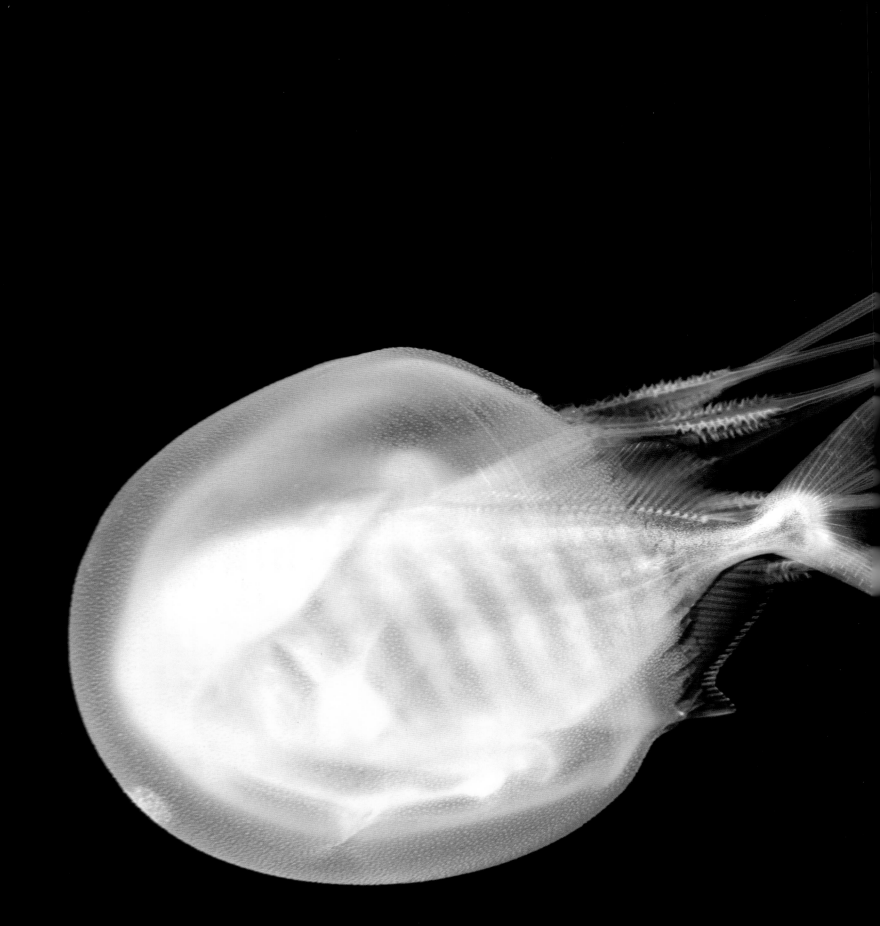

Jack hiding in a Jellyfish

Family Carangidae and Genus *Thysanostoma*,
both species unknown

This 3 inch long (7.6 cm) juvenile jack hides in a 10 inch
(25 cm) scyphozoan jelly with its purple, rope-like tentacles. For a time, the jack is small enough to fit into the
jellyfish, and the association gives the jack protection
from predators. Soon, however, the jack will grow up and
grow out of this close relationship.

Tropical Two-wing Flying Fish

Exocoetus volitans, probable species

This juvenile flying fish, 5 inches long (12.5 cm), swims only inches below the surface, feeding on crustaceans and other plankton. To escape predators, it will break through the surface to glide over the waves. This species is extraordinarily numerous across the circumtropical ocean; the population has been estimated at more than one billion individuals.

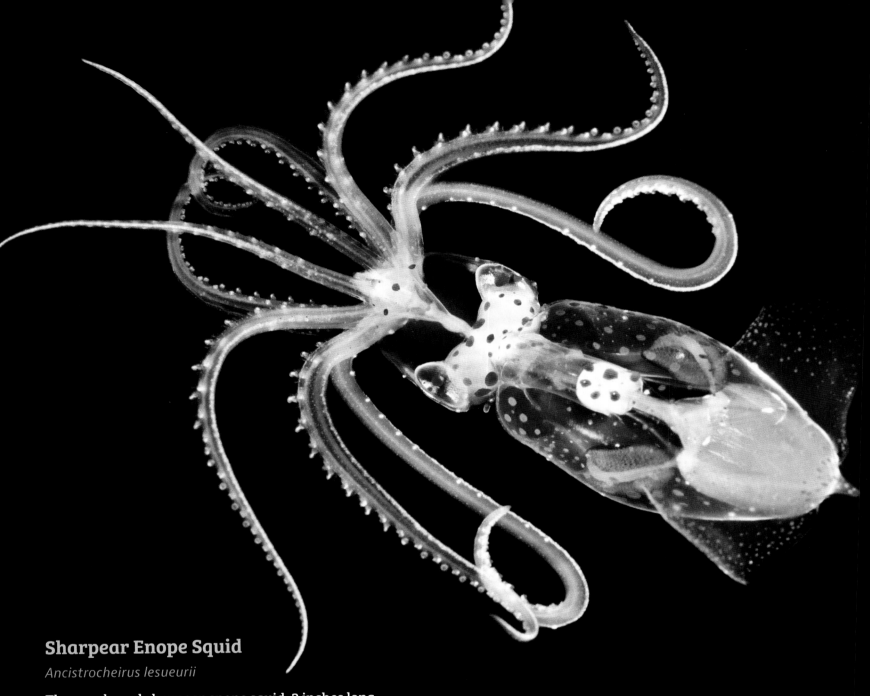

Sharpear Enope Squid

Ancistrocheirus lesueurii

The paralarval sharpear enope squid, 2 inches long
(5 cm), comes to the surface at night. Adults reach a
length of 15 ½ inches (39 cm), not including the two tentacles and eight arms, and are usually found in food-rich
slope habitats near the ocean floor. They live throughout
the tropical and subtropical ocean where they try to
avoid their predators, including sperm whales, boarfish
and large pelagic sharks.

Cusk Eel

Brotulotaenia nielseni

This 2 inch long (5 cm) larval fish has elaborate dorsal-
and anal-fin rays. Some researchers have described them
as looking like a seabird feather, but in the water, the
larval form more closely resembles *Forskalia* siphonophores. This mimicry might deter predators that avoid
stinging siphonophores.

Arm Squid
Brachioteuthis, species unknown

Arm squids in the paralarval stage have a unique elongated neck held in place by hydrostatic pressure coming from a fluid-filled sac in the mantle. No one knows the purpose of this special feature but when the 1 ½ inch (3.8 cm) paralarva matures to the adult stage at 6 inches (15 cm), the neck disappears. Arm squid paralarvae hatch from tiny free-floating eggs only up to about ³⁄₆₄ inch long (1.2 mm). They live entirely in the upper 656 feet (200 m) of the sea.

Longjaw Flounder (right)
Chascanopsetta prorigera

The adult of this 4 inch long (10 cm) larval flounder has a protruding lower jaw that gives it its name. In the larval stage, the eyes are positioned on either side of its head, like most fish, but as it matures, the eyes move to the left side of the body. As an adult, this flounder will abandon its vertical migrations and take up residence lying on its side camouflaged on the bottom, waiting to ambush its small fish and crustacean prey.

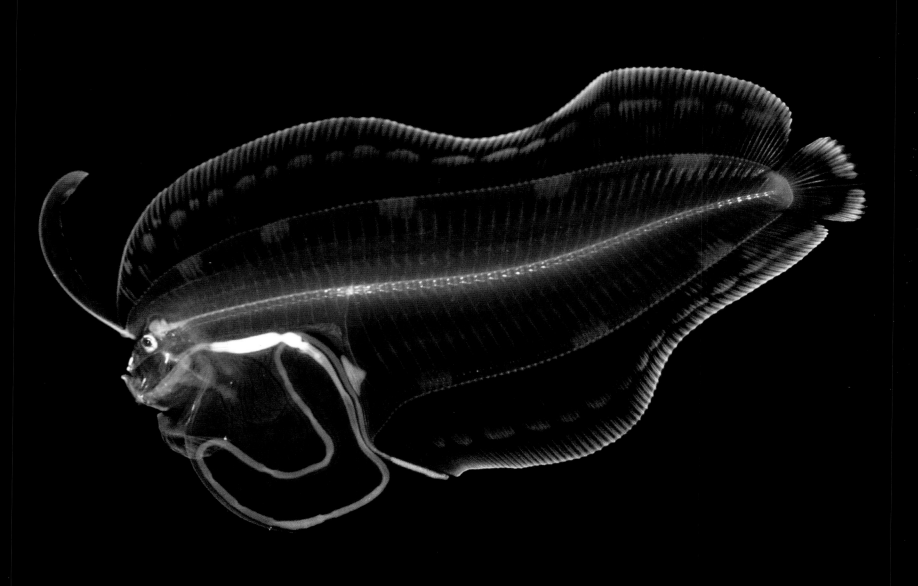

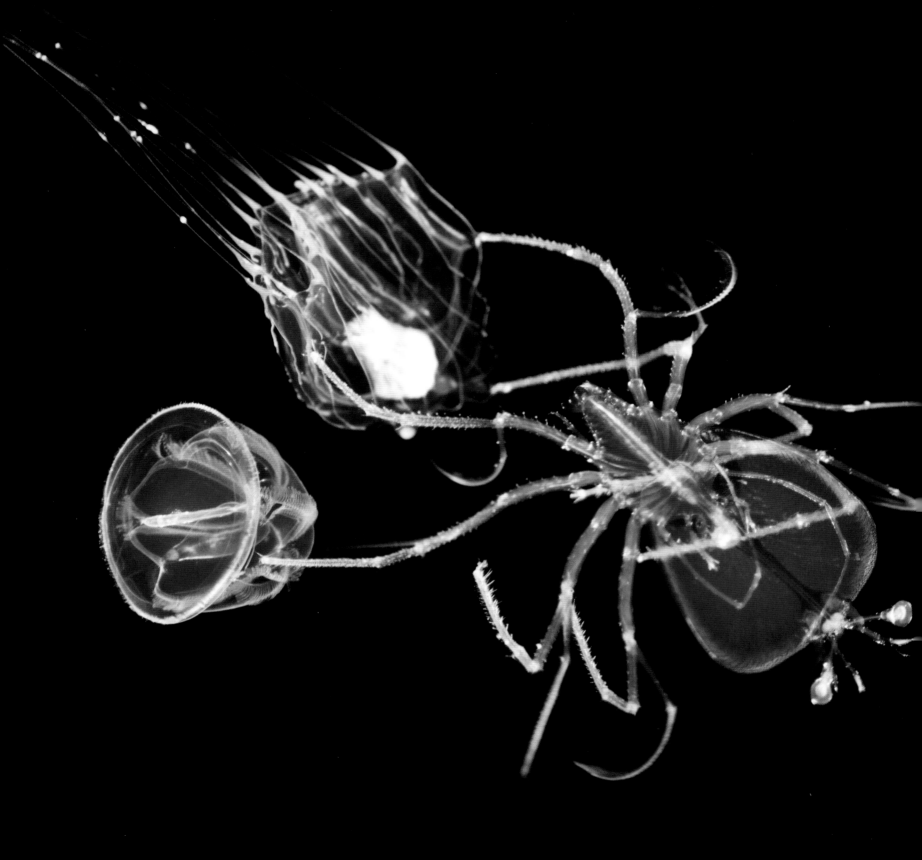

Lobster riding a Mauve Stinger

Unknown Lobster species
with *Pelagia noctiluca*

This larval lobster, about an inch long
(2.5 cm) and still in the phyllosoma
stage, uses its legs to ride on or carry
a mauve stinger. Any overly curious
predators will get a mouthful of purple
tentacles with stinging nematocysts for
its trouble. Is the lobster's main purpose
to ride on or carry a jellyfish for defense
or is it a food source? It is mainly, if not
only, defense.

Lobster carrying Acorn Worm and Anthomedusa (left)

Unknown Lobster with Acorn Worm
species and *Merga*, species unknown

This larval lobster in the phyllosoma
stage, only half an inch long (1.3 cm),
carries its defense shield and perhaps its
lunch. The acorn worm is in the larval
stage called tornaria. Acorn worms are
in fact hemichordates, not segmented
worms, and are closely related to echino-
derms. When mature, they move into the
seabed, burying themselves in the sand.
The anthomedusa *Merga* is a kind of
hydrozoan and one of only eight related
species found in Hawaiian waters.

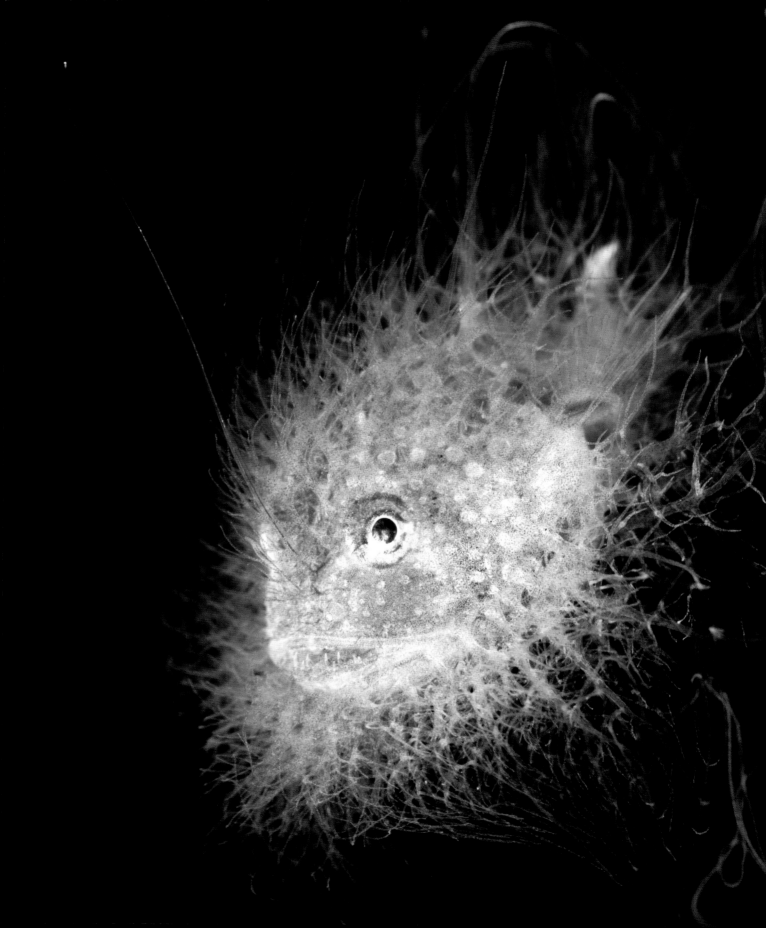

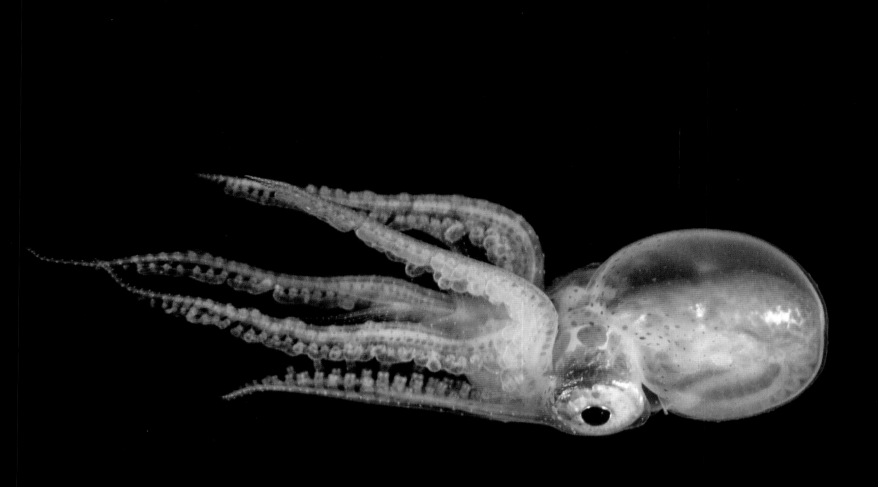

Hairy Goosefish (left)

Lophiodes fimbriatus

In 2017, Sarah Matye called biologist-photographer Jeff Milisen over to check out an exotic-looking jellyfish, about 1 inch long (2.5 cm). Looking closer, Jeff noticed "it has eyes and fins!" It turned out to be a subadult hairy goosefish, like the one pictured here, which had been found only in Japan in 1985 but was now turning up in Hawai'i. When it is seen swimming in surface waters or drifting over the sandy bottom, the hairy goosefish mimics jellies, the scyphozoans.

Blanket Octopus

Tremoctopus, species unknown, probably *Tremoctopus gracilis*

This portrait of a young male blanket octopus, less than an inch long (2.5 cm), is probably in the paralarval stage. The male blanket octopus is dwarfed by the giant female that grows up to 6 ½ feet long (2 m) (see pages 64–65). Despite its small size, the male can be fierce, known to rip the tentacles from Portuguese man o' war and wave them around to keep off would-be predators. Like many other octopus species, they can dispatch ink into the water to confuse predators.

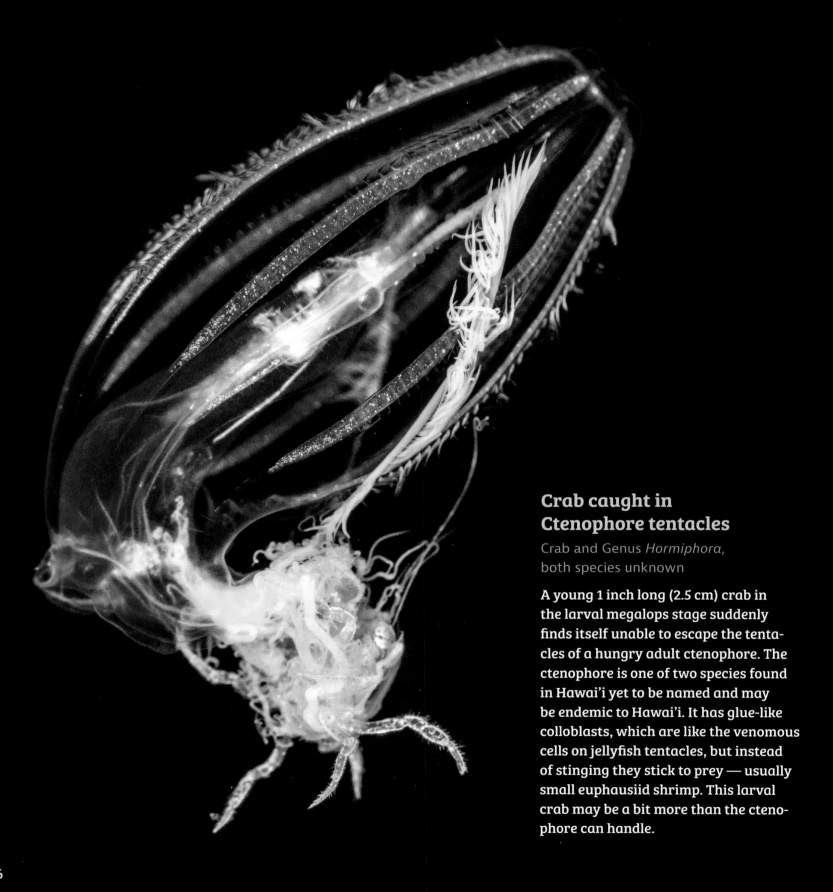

Crab caught in Ctenophore tentacles

Crab and Genus *Hormiphora*, both species unknown

A young 1 inch long (2.5 cm) crab in the larval megalops stage suddenly finds itself unable to escape the tentacles of a hungry adult ctenophore. The ctenophore is one of two species found in Hawai'i yet to be named and may be endemic to Hawai'i. It has glue-like colloblasts, which are like the venomous cells on jellyfish tentacles, but instead of stinging they stick to prey — usually small euphausiid shrimp. This larval crab may be a bit more than the ctenophore can handle.

Venus Girdle

Cestum veneris

This adult ctenophore, or comb jelly, measuring 1 foot (30.5 cm) across, feeds on copepods and small crustaceans. When alarmed, the Venus girdle undulates to get away using its cilia to create movement. If the danger persists, it curls up into a spiral to protect the vulnerable central part of its body, including its sensitive feeding mouth.

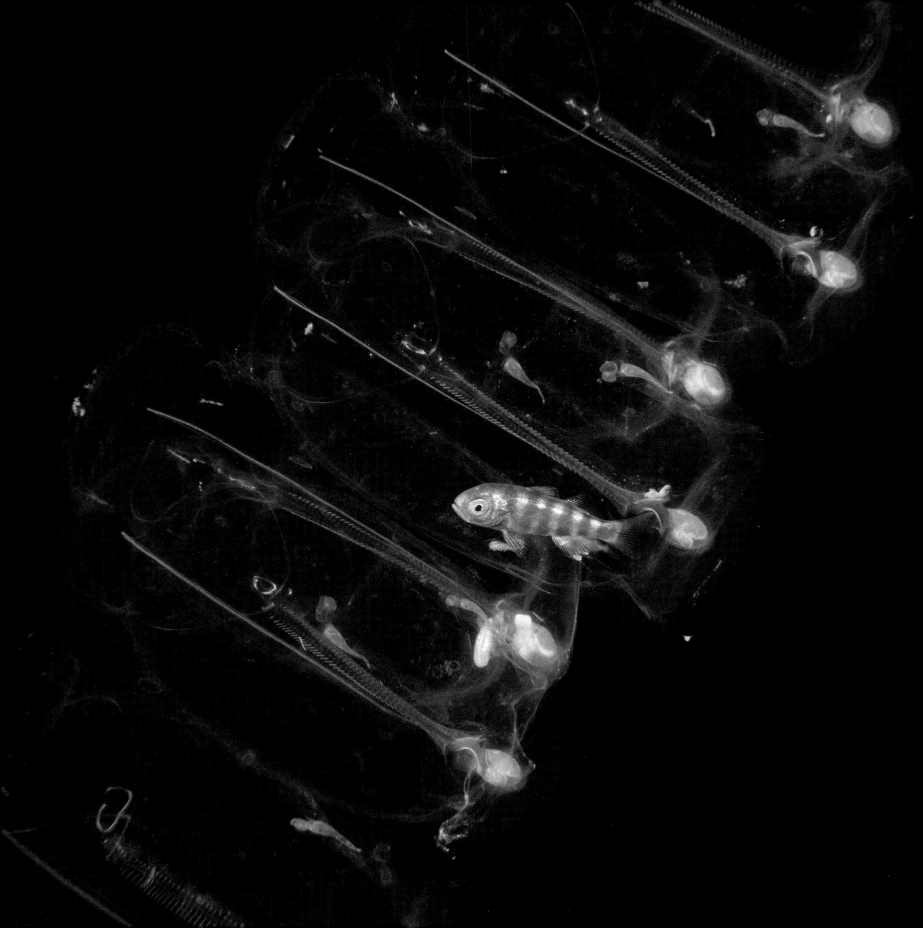

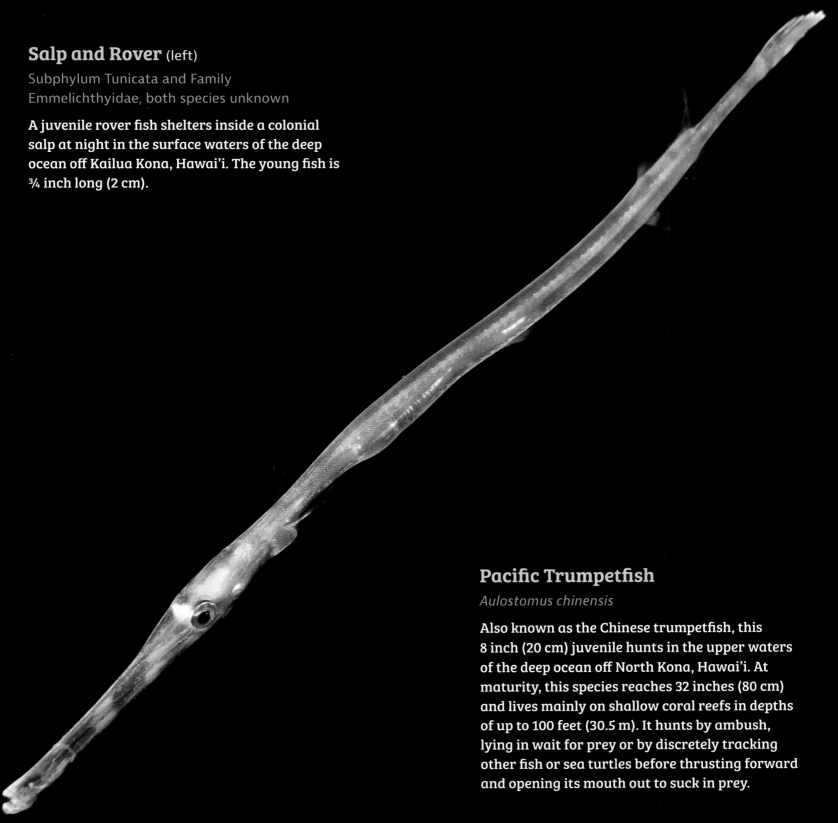

Salp and Rover (left)

Subphylum Tunicata and Family
Emmelichthyidae, both species unknown

A juvenile rover fish shelters inside a colonial
salp at night in the surface waters of the deep
ocean off Kailua Kona, Hawai'i. The young fish is
¾ inch long (2 cm).

Pacific Trumpetfish

Aulostomus chinensis

Also known as the Chinese trumpetfish, this
8 inch (20 cm) juvenile hunts in the upper waters
of the deep ocean off North Kona, Hawai'i. At
maturity, this species reaches 32 inches (80 cm)
and lives mainly on shallow coral reefs in depths
of up to 100 feet (30.5 m). It hunts by ambush,
lying in wait for prey or by discretely tracking
other fish or sea turtles before thrusting forward
and opening its mouth out to suck in prey.

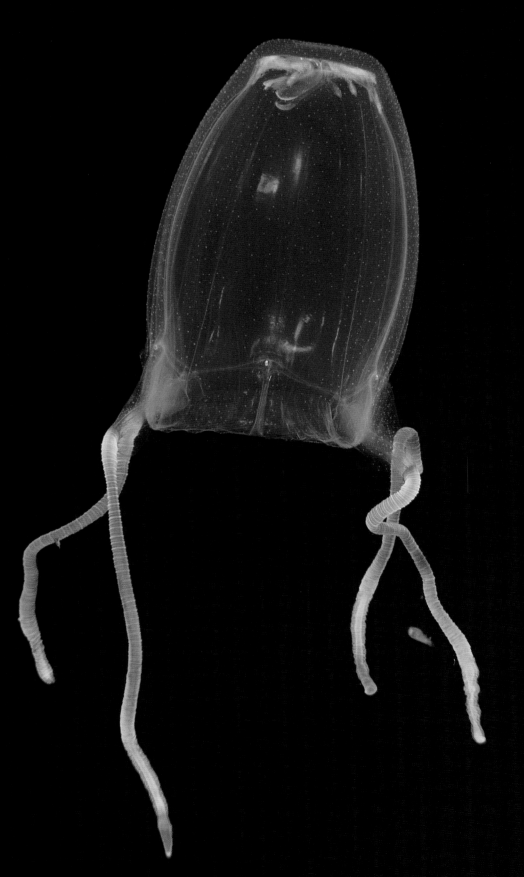

Box Jellyfish
Alatina alata

This box jellyfish species lives inshore as well as offshore in global tropical waters. It's sometimes called a sea wasp, but it's not the classic sea wasp or Australian box jelly, *Chironex fleckeri.* This one, about 8 inches long (20 cm), was discovered at night in the deep surface waters off Kailua Kona. The four tentacles carry bands of nematocysts along their length, capable of killing prey that bump into them and causing severe stinging pain to humans. It can take 20 minutes to a day or more to recover from a box jellyfish encounter.

Pram Bug and Tunicate

Genus *Phronima* and Subphylum Tunicata (Order Salpida or Doliolida), both species unknown

Carrying a clutch of eggs, this adult female pram bug, 1 9/16 inch (4 cm), has just invaded a 3 1/8 inch (8 cm) salp or doliolid tunicate in the warm nighttime waters off Kona, Hawai'i. The pram bug will feed on the internal organs of the tunicate to hollow it out, then lay her eggs inside the salp. When the eggs hatch, the young pram bugs feed on the remainder of the tunicate until they are ready to leave and find their own tunicate to exploit and live in.

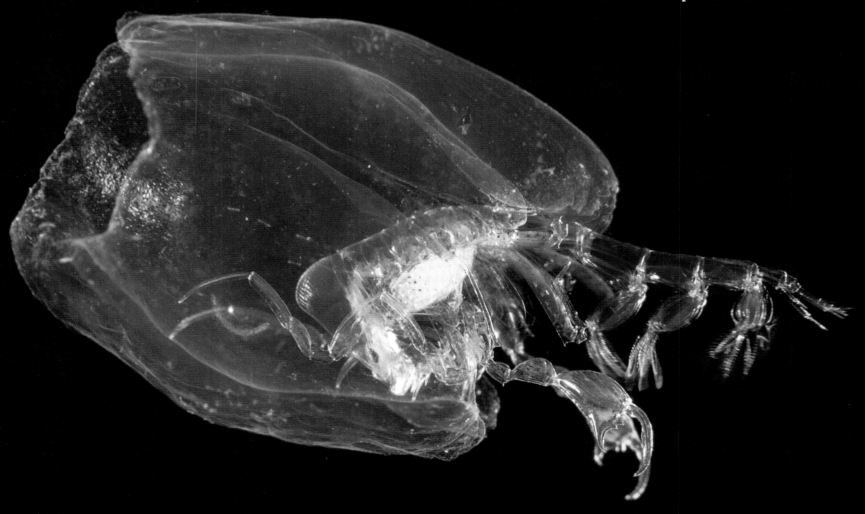

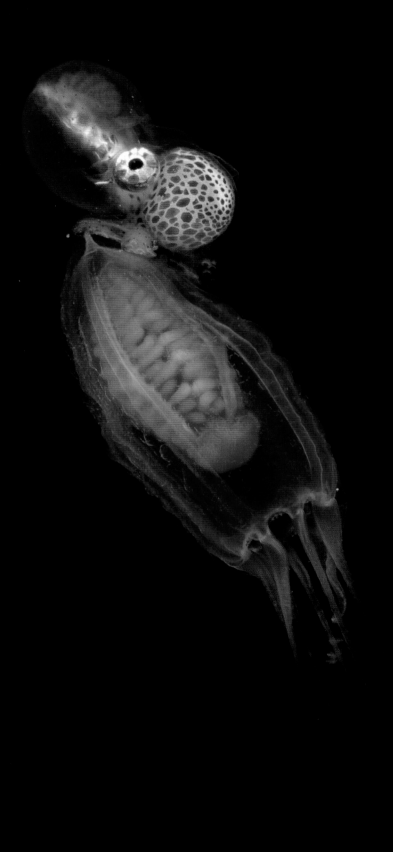

CHAPTER 3

Awesome Anilao

"Time evaporates when you're blackwater diving," says diver-photographer Mike Bartick. "You're looking through the viewfinder, focusing on specks of plankton, and it's easy to drift and go deeper. You have to pay attention to your ears and to the little computer on your arm to watch your depth. You need a third eye to keep track of the light on the safety line."

Mike started bluewater diving off southern California before visiting the Philippines and falling in love with Anilao. When divers first started coming to Anilao, it was just the name of a township. In recent years, the whole peninsula, flanked by two deep bays — Balayan Bay to the west and Batangas Bay to the east plus Marikaban Island — is referred to as Anilao. The two bays are open to the even deeper waters of the Verde Island Passage, separating the main Luzon Island from Mindoro Island and opening into the South China Sea. These flowing waters of the Verde Island Passage provide a source of nutrients for the bays and that has led to the diverse marine life. The South China Sea all along the western Philippine archipelago has its own oceanography separate from the North Pacific Subtropical Gyre and the other main Pacific basin currents. The seas here are often flat and almost calm except during the annual four months of typhoon season.

Perched at the apex of the Coral Triangle, Anilao and the two bays also form a central part of the Verde Island Passage Marine Protected Area Network, with more than 60 marine protected areas (MPAs). The Coral Triangle, the "Amazon of the seas," extends south to Indonesia and East to Papua New Guinea and the Solomon Islands. It stands as a global hotspot for biodiversity with 76% of the world's

« **Paper nautilus riding a jellyfish**

shallow water reef-building coral species and 37% of its reef fish species.

Mike hosts divers at his resort in Anilao, but he often visits other sites in the Coral Triangle and further afield in the North Pacific, the Atlantic and the Caribbean. Each site has its own specialties along with species in common, including deepwater fish that follow the plankton into the shallower part of the mesopelagic zone.

"Anilao is not as deep as off Hawai'i's Kona coast," says Mike. "A few hundred feet up to 1,500 feet (450 m) in the channels. We dive in at least 500 feet (150 m), usually more.

When we first went night diving in Anilao, some people said it's not true blackwater diving with vertical migrators, but then they saw the photographs we were getting."

The invertebrate species attracting particular attention include the paper nautilus, the blanket octopus and the diamond squid.

Mike says it's not just vertical migration that's going on. Some plankton get caught up in currents and are pushed along horizontally. When he goes diving in California, he now stays closer to shore, where before he went up to 10 miles (16 km) out to dive above the

The male blanket octopus, tiny but able to rip off jellyfish tentacles to defend itself

continental shelf. Of course, places like Monterey Bay have a lot of vertical migration going on close to shore with the Monterey Canyon extending down to 5,000 feet (1,520 m). But even shallower areas can be rich in sea life.

"Plankton are some of the smallest organisms in the world that play some of the biggest roles," says Mike. "These tiny organisms carry the weight of the planet on their shoulders. People just don't know. You mention the word 'plankton' — I love doing this in a talk — and instantly their eyes glaze over, but you try to tell people 'you can thank plankton for every other breath. They cleanse the carbon, and they get no thanks.'"

On his travels and with the developing network of the Blackwater Photo Group he started, Mike is eager to encourage more divers and diving companies to try blackwater diving.

"The deep ocean is kind of like the eighth continent and the biggest one too. Why do people spend so much time going to national parks when we have the ocean on our doorstep with the kelp forest and the beautiful wonder that is there? Problem is that if you look across the ocean, there's nothing to see except a sailboat — it looks like a desert. But when you stick your head under the water, it's just this unbelievable place that's completely wild."

Diamond squid are slow swimmers with one of the fastest growth rates of all squid

A Typical Blackwater Dive

"If I focus on the large stuff, I'll miss the small stuff," says Mike Bartick. Here's what the world of one photographer and the vertical migrators at night look like in a single cubic yard, or meter, of ocean — about the size of a small cooking stove.

"On a typical blackwater dive, a lot of the stuff is so small it just looks like snow in the water. As I move in, it starts to get larger and more visible to the naked eye. I see small jellyfish moving around, comb jellies and some pulsating jellies. In addition to the down lights, I aim my torch with a tight beam to look through the water column.

"After a while, I get used to it; everything seems to be moving at the same speed in one direction. I don't notice it because I'm going with it, but then I might see something move in a different direction. It catches my eye — only because you do it so long your brain is trained for shape recognition, movement and contrast. From everything being white or transparent, you might see something that is a little more opaque and then it might move and you look at it and it's small and it could be an ornate fish or worm.

"And then some of the even smaller stuff catches your eye — just beautiful — like the veliger snail. The foot of this snail is like somebody rolled it in sequins, in glitter. And you have to think what purpose does this serve for this animal?

"When you are looking at a small scale, you can see all these little details of nature and how they are tied together. And you glimpse how the subject works its way through the plankton until it's old enough and strong enough to finally settle. And then you start expanding out and of course you see the larger fish taking more space. But the smaller organisms don't require much space. They're just fluttering around in this cube of water and that could be their entire world for however long their life cycle is.

"But even in this cubic yard of water, they are all pulsing, moving up and down. For some it must be equivalent to scaling the height of Mt. Everest and back every day to get here. When they are all moving together and you're underwater and you're looking, you might not really notice the immediate water around you. You have to look close to see and to try to sample things out of it. It can be quite difficult, especially to see the smallest organisms. You shoot away with your camera and then pray that the photographs are sharp. And then topside you spend a lot of time looking at each image and figuring out the species you've been photographing."

Thorny seahorse grabbing sea grass

Paper Nautilus with Jellyfish

Argonauta hians (probable) with *Eutiara decorata*

The paper nautilus often rides jellyfish, but this mature male nautilus, only ½ inch (1.3 cm), is not only riding on but also thought to be pulling a jellyfish twice his size, 1 inch long (2.5 cm). The propulsive force is generated by the spouting from the funnel of the paper nautilus. A type of small octopus, the nautilus acts similarly to an octopus on the seabed but instead of hiding in the rocks, it often hides in a jellyfish. Some paper nautiluses cut holes in the jellyfish's umbrella-shaped mantle, or bell, to enable them to siphon food from the jellyfish's gut.

Octopus

Species unknown

This larval octopus, with its transparent mantle less than ¾ of an inch (1.8 cm) across, is a species whose larvae have not yet been associated with their adult forms. It may even be a species as yet unknown to science. Similar-looking larval individuals grow up to be a wunderpus octopus or a mimic octopus, but this one has a different arm length and suction cup arrangement. To find out its identity as an adult, biologists need to take and analyze genetic samples or raise an individual from larva to adult stage.

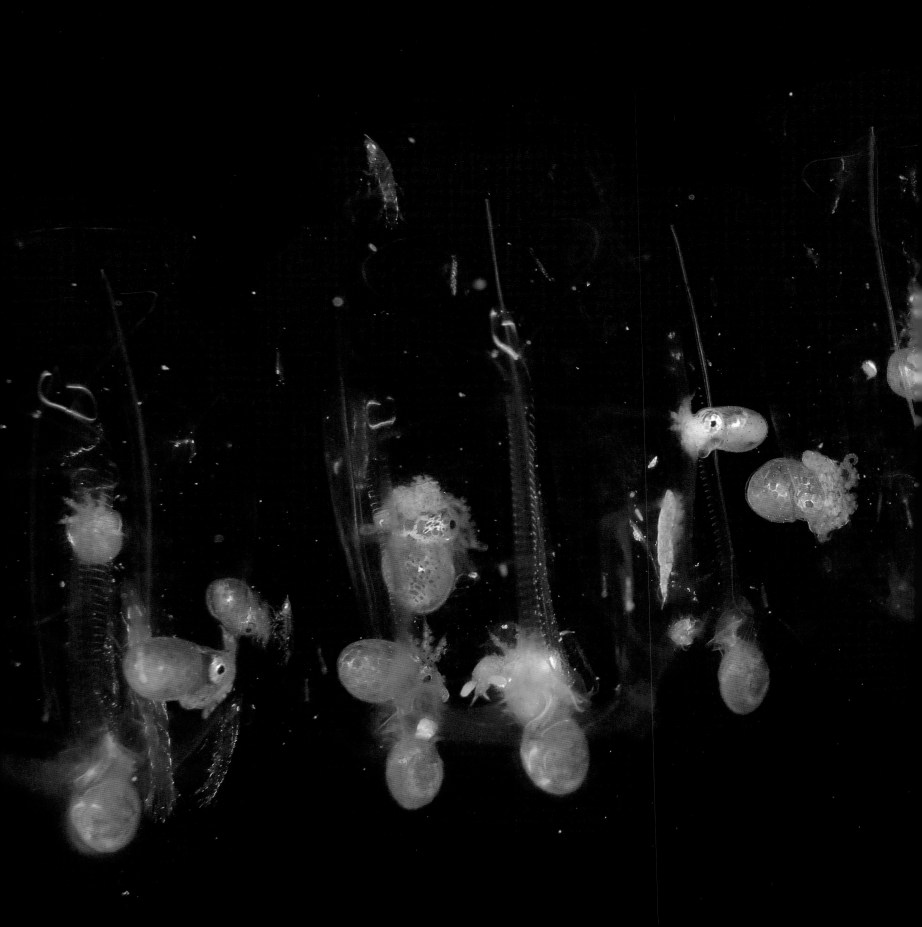

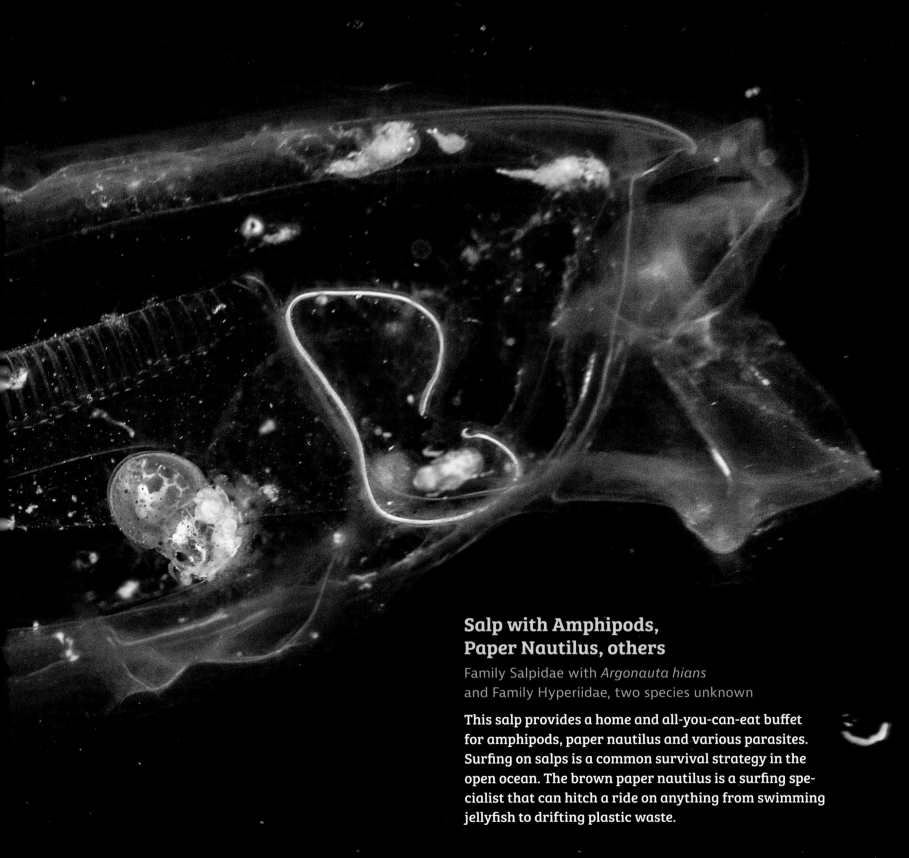

Salp with Amphipods, Paper Nautilus, others

Family Salpidae with *Argonauta hians*
and Family Hyperiidae, two species unknown

This salp provides a home and all-you-can-eat buffet for amphipods, paper nautilus and various parasites. Surfing on salps is a common survival strategy in the open ocean. The brown paper nautilus is a surfing specialist that can hitch a ride on anything from swimming jellyfish to drifting plastic waste.

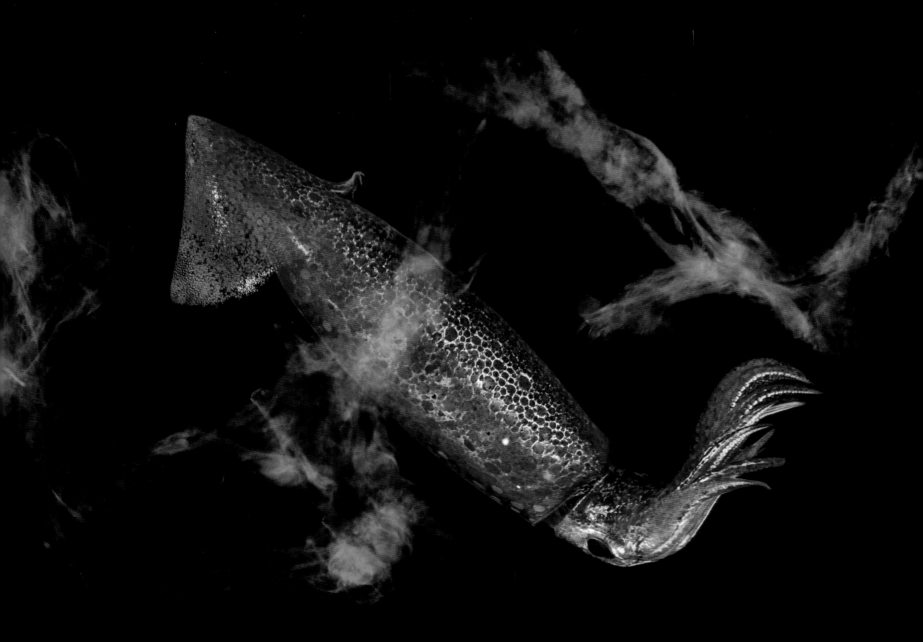

Neon Flying Squid
Ommastrephes bartramii

In Balayan Bay off Anilao, squid ink, a defense mechanism, spills into the nighttime sea. Sometimes called the red flying squid, this species reaches a length of 17 ¾ inches (45 cm) for males and 35 ½ inches (90 cm) for females.

Sea Angels (right)
Hydromyles globulosus

Sea angels meet and mate in Balayan Bay. Each measuring about ⅜ inch (1 cm), these naked (shell-less) pelagic snails, or pteropods, are translucent with tentacles and a wing-like protrusion, which is a modified snail foot. Unlike most egg-laying invertebrates, this species has offspring that develop inside its body and it then gives birth to live young.

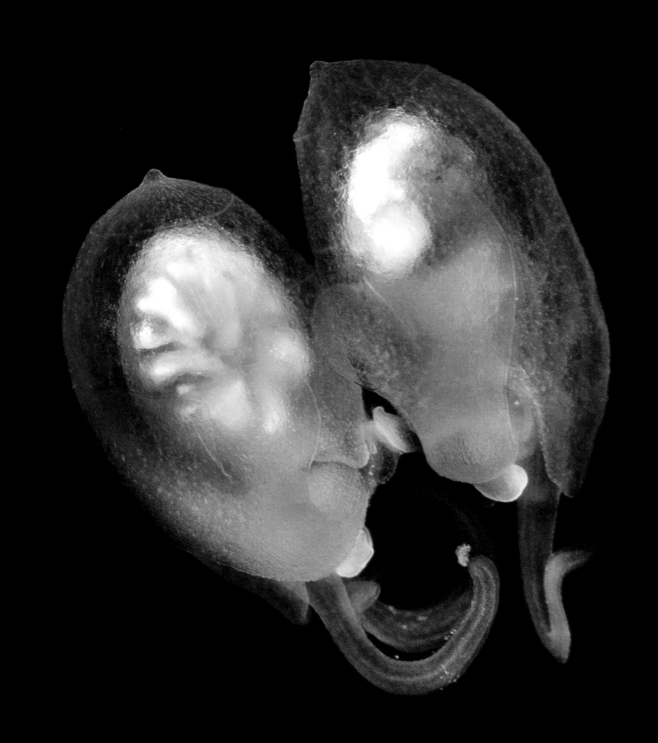

Longhorn Cowfish
Lactoria cornuta

A juvenile longhorn cowfish, ¾ inch long (2 cm), swims out in the open ocean of Balayan Bay, Anilao. As adults, growing up to 20 inches long (50 cm), they settle on or near the bottom, often on coral reefs. They eat both plants and animals, including benthic algae, various microorganisms and the single-celled foraminiferans that they strain from sediments. They also eat sponges, polychaete worms from sand flats, mollusks, small crustaceans and small fish. They are able to find benthic invertebrates for food by blowing jets of water into the sandy substrate.

Anemone

Order Actiniaria, species unknown

A larval anemone floats in the open ocean waters of Balayan Bay, Anilao. These flowerlike marine, predatory animals are named after the flowering anemone plant because of their colorful appearance. They are a close relative of coral and jellyfish.

Rover and Pyrosomes

Family Emmelichthyidae and
Genus *Pyrosoma*, species unknown

This juvenile rover has moved into a colony of pyrosomes, free-floating colonial tunicates that live in the warm open ocean in Balayan Bay, Anilao. As adults, rovers are found in the ocean's twilight zone, the near-deep water layer where light is dim. Pyrosomes are colonial pelagic tuni- cates, which are closely related to salps and that live in tube-shaped colonies that can be large. Pyrosome means "fire body," from their ability to produce bright bioluminescence.

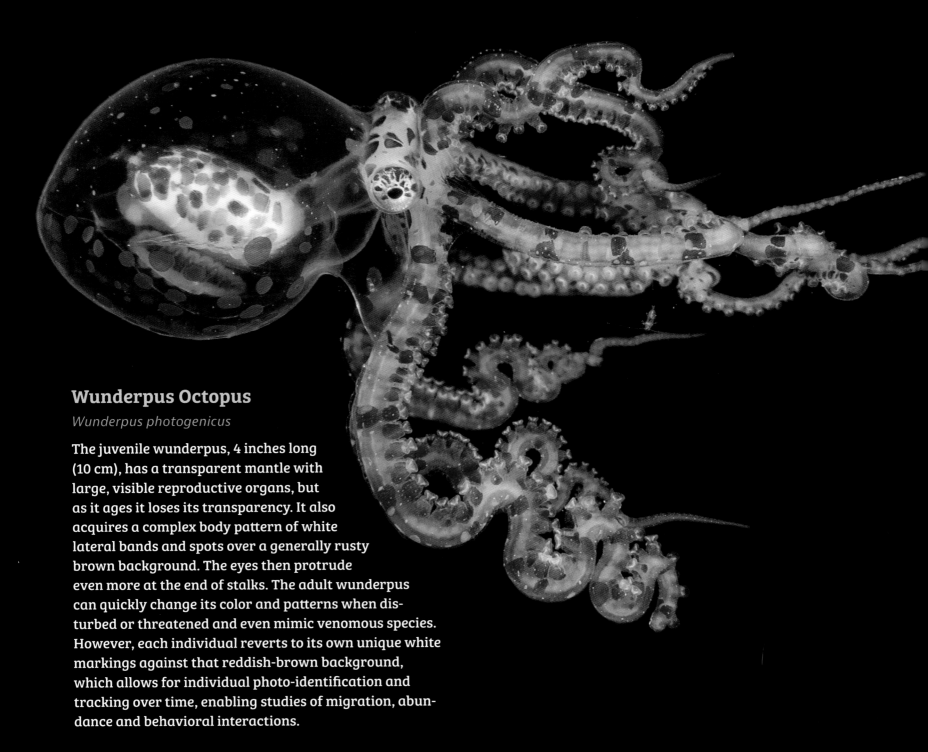

Wunderpus Octopus

Wunderpus photogenicus

The juvenile wunderpus, 4 inches long
(10 cm), has a transparent mantle with
large, visible reproductive organs, but
as it ages it loses its transparency. It also
acquires a complex body pattern of white
lateral bands and spots over a generally rusty
brown background. The eyes then protrude
even more at the end of stalks. The adult wunderpus
can quickly change its color and patterns when disturbed or threatened and even mimic venomous species.
However, each individual reverts to its own unique white
markings against that reddish-brown background,
which allows for individual photo-identification and
tracking over time, enabling studies of migration, abundance and behavioral interactions.

Paper Nautilus and Tunicate

Argonauta hians and Genus *Pyrosoma*, species unknown

A female paper nautilus drifts through the ocean night off Anilao on its free-floating colonial tunicate platform.

Surgeonfish (right)

Family Acanthuridae, species unknown

This juvenile surgeonfish is a nighttime visitor to Balayan Bay off Anilao. It sports the common transparent and somewhat spiky appearance of the juvenile whose nightly visits to the surface waters require some protection from predators.

Blanket Octopus
Tremoctopus gracilis

The blanket octopus resides in tropical and subtropical seas. This male, found off Anilao, measures 1 inch long (2.5 cm). In this species, the male is dwarfed by the female. The female has expanded webs, called blankets. Blanket octopodes are immune to the venomous Portuguese man o' war, whose tentacles the male and immature females rip off and use for defensive purposes.

Sharpear Enope Squid

Ancistrocheirus lesueurii

A juvenile sharpear enope squid, ¼ inch long (0.6 cm), poses momentarily for the photographer, night diving off Anilao. This species is usually found alone or in pairs, highly animated though not swimming in shoals like other squid. This one was found 75 feet (23.2 m) down in an area more than 500 feet (150 m) deep.

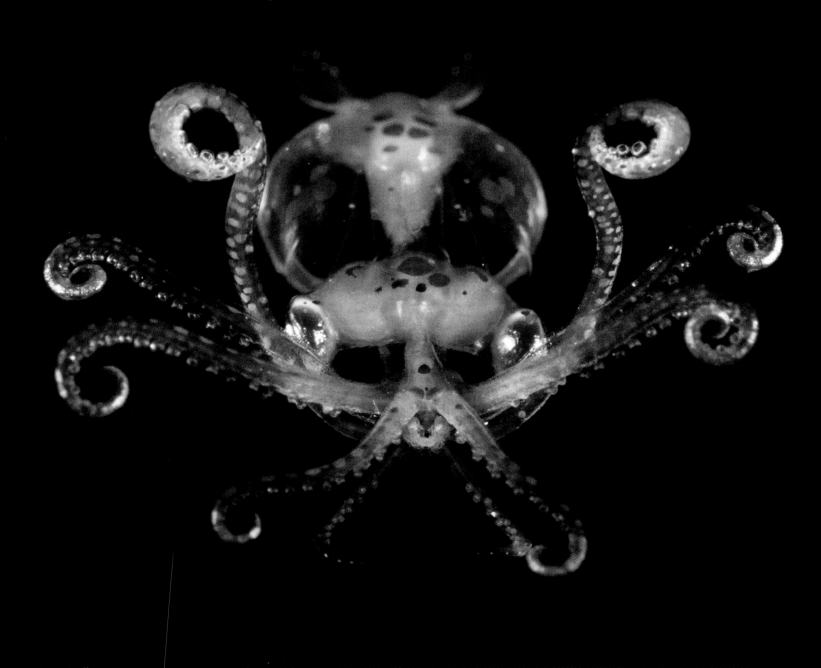

Blanket Octopus

Tremoctopus gracilis

The female blanket octopus is a formidable sight. Female blanket octopuses can reach a size of 6 ½ feet (2 m), and they are 10,000 to 40,000 times heavier than the males. Few species show such a great size difference between males and females.

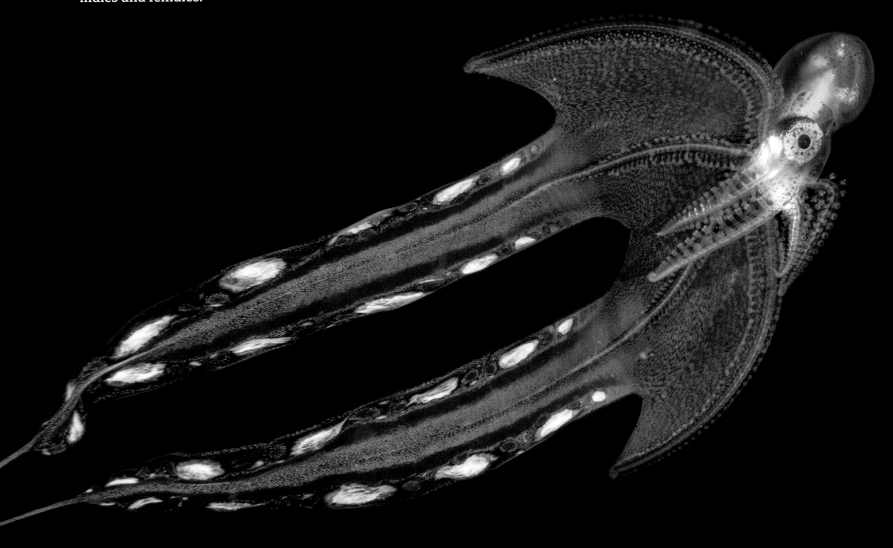

Snake Blenny

Family Blenniidae, tribe Nemophin, species unknown

In the waters of Balayan Bay, Anilao, this 2 inch (5 cm) larval fish is thought to be a snake blenny, possibly *Xiphasia setifer*. It often swims backwards and forwards like the motion of a snake crawling.

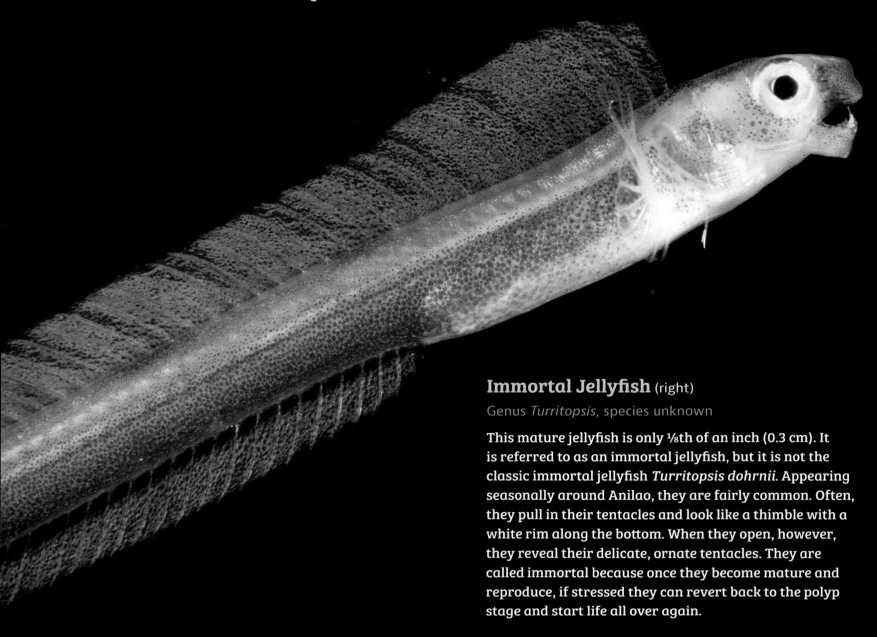

Immortal Jellyfish (right)

Genus *Turritopsis*, species unknown

This mature jellyfish is only ⅛th of an inch (0.3 cm). It is referred to as an immortal jellyfish, but it is not the classic immortal jellyfish *Turritopsis dohrnii*. Appearing seasonally around Anilao, they are fairly common. Often, they pull in their tentacles and look like a thimble with a white rim along the bottom. When they open, however, they reveal their delicate, ornate tentacles. They are called immortal because once they become mature and reproduce, if stressed they can revert back to the polyp stage and start life all over again.

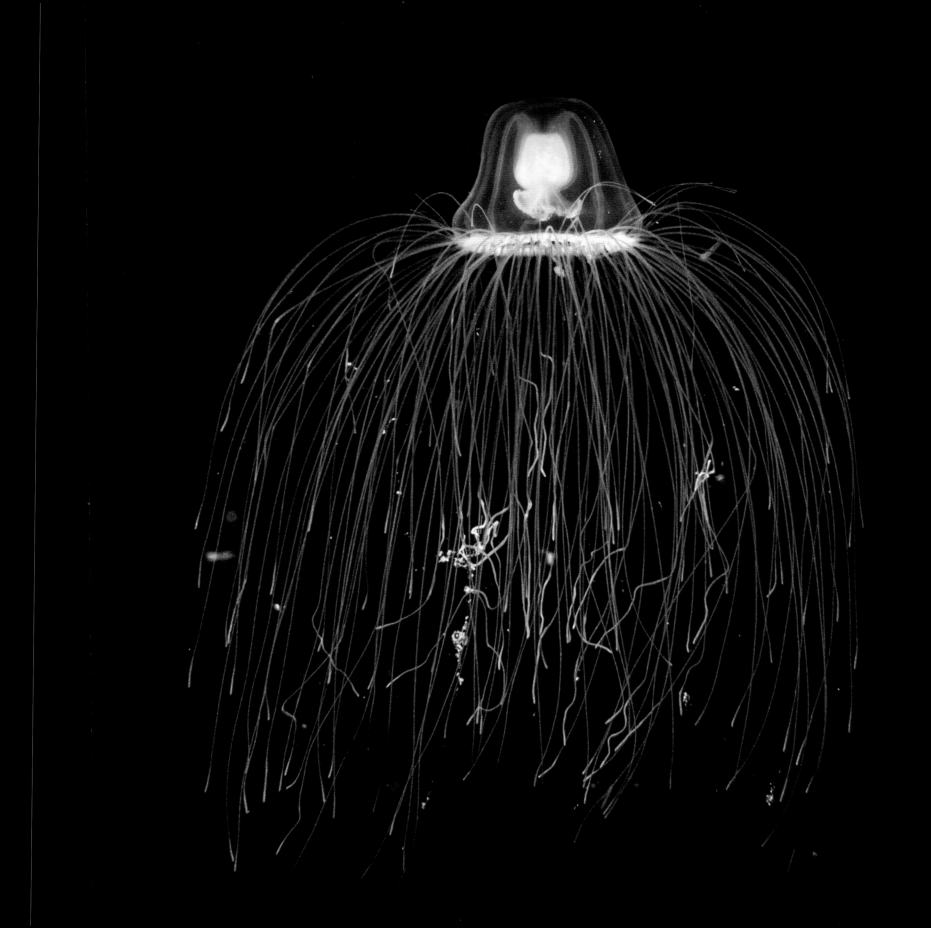

Amphipod eating an Ant

Order Amphipoda, species unknown

Amphipods are known to be scavengers, but this ¼ inch
(0.6 cm) amphipod has the catch of its life — a winged ant
that may have landed in the water following a nuptial
flight. It happened one night when Mike Bartick photographed an amphipod spiraling down to where he was
diving, about 20 feet (6 m) below the surface. It
looked like it was carrying something reddish
and odd. Only later when he saw the photograph did he realize that it was an ant.

Mantis Shrimp, or Stomatopod

Order Stomatopoda, species unknown

With its big glassy eyes and transparent body, this larval creature, ½ inch long (1.3 cm), belongs to one of the more than 400 species of mantis shrimp, or stomatopods, but exact species identifications of mantis shrimp larvae are difficult.

Sea Slug or Marine Gastropod Mollusk

Family Pleurobranchidae, species unknown

This ⅛ inch (0.3 cm) individual, part of the plankton, is an example of Pleurobranch veliger. Veliger is the larval stage in sea slugs, but the species remains unknown. This photograph was taken some 45 feet (13.7 cm) below the surface.

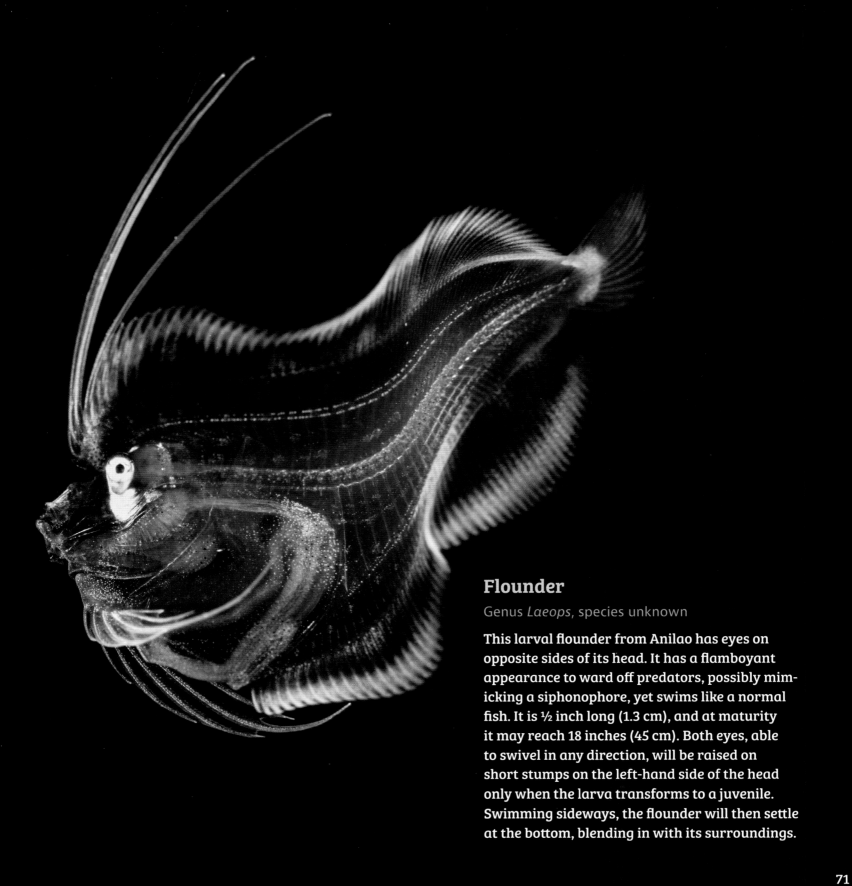

Flounder

Genus *Laeops*, species unknown

This larval flounder from Anilao has eyes on
opposite sides of its head. It has a flamboyant
appearance to ward off predators, possibly mim-
icking a siphonophore, yet swims like a normal
fish. It is ½ inch long (1.3 cm), and at maturity
it may reach 18 inches (45 cm). Both eyes, able
to swivel in any direction, will be raised on
short stumps on the left-hand side of the head
only when the larva transforms to a juvenile.
Swimming sideways, the flounder will then settle
at the bottom, blending in with its surroundings.

71

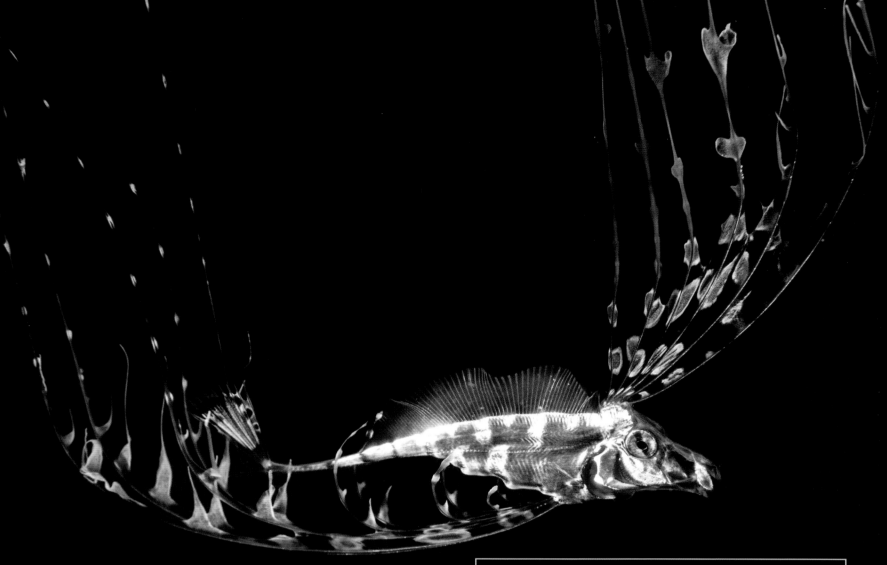

Scalloped Ribbonfish

Zu cristatus

The 1 inch (2.5 cm) juvenile ribbonfish shown here, photographed in Anilao, has up to 1 foot long (30.5 cm) appendages that give its predators the forbidding impression of stinging jelly tentacles. As an adult, maximum length of nearly 4 feet — 46.5 inches (118 cm) — it retires to the deep mesopelagic zone. Ribbonfish are found worldwide in tropical to temperate waters of pelagic seas. Some fish in this order, the oarfishes, are thought to reach 30 feet (9 m) in length.

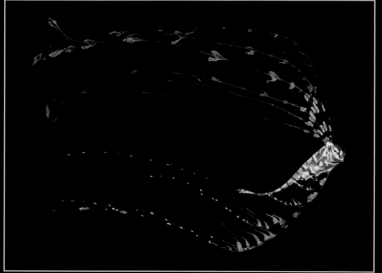

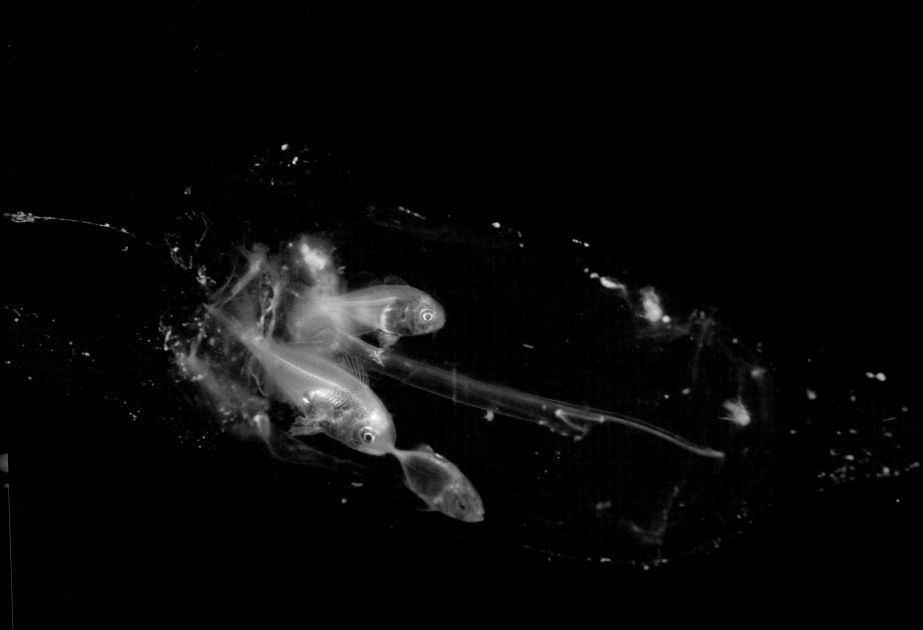

Salp sheltering Driftfish

Family Salpidae and Genus *Cubiceps*, species unknown

Forty feet (12.2 m) down in Janao Bay, Anilao, this 4 inch
(10 cm) salp, a barrel-shaped tunicate, provides a home
for a number of organisms — including this larval
driftfish, only about ¼ inch long (0.6 cm). The young
driftfish are thus mostly protected from passing predator plankton.

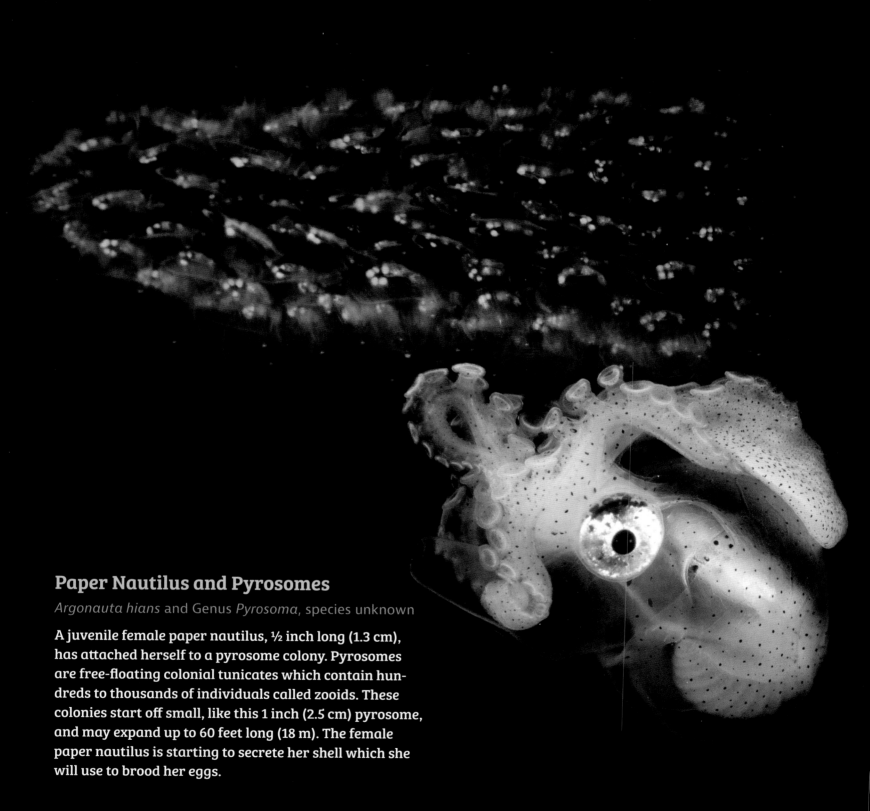

Paper Nautilus and Pyrosomes

Argonauta hians and Genus *Pyrosoma*, species unknown

A juvenile female paper nautilus, ½ inch long (1.3 cm), has attached herself to a pyrosome colony. Pyrosomes are free-floating colonial tunicates which contain hundreds to thousands of individuals called zooids. These colonies start off small, like this 1 inch (2.5 cm) pyrosome, and may expand up to 60 feet long (18 m). The female paper nautilus is starting to secrete her shell which she will use to brood her eggs.

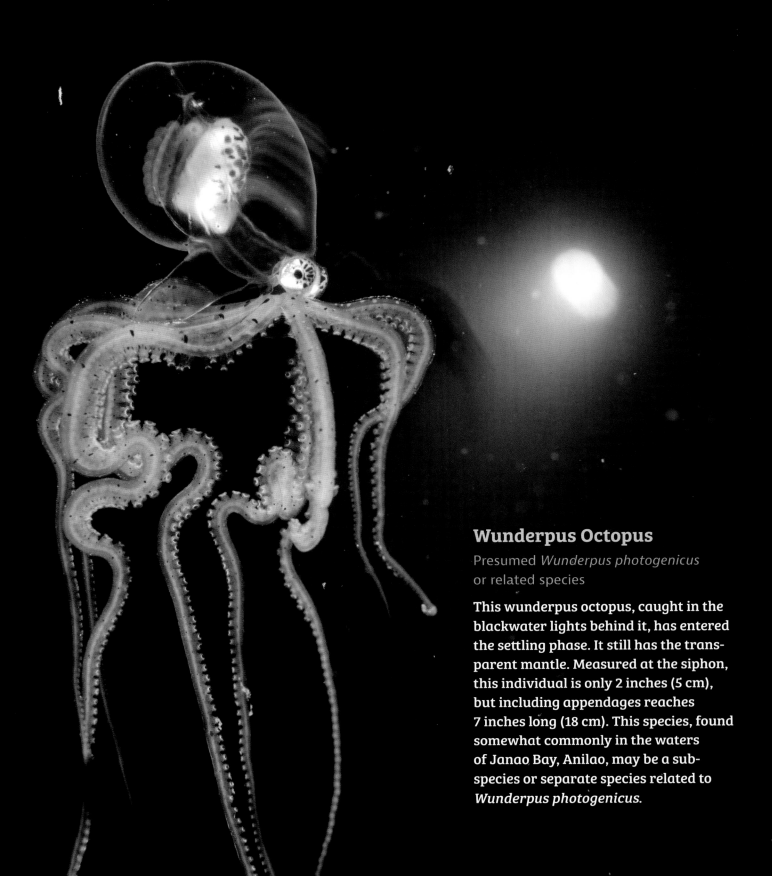

Wunderpus Octopus

Presumed *Wunderpus photogenicus* or related species

This wunderpus octopus, caught in the blackwater lights behind it, has entered the settling phase. It still has the transparent mantle. Measured at the siphon, this individual is only 2 inches (5 cm), but including appendages reaches 7 inches long (18 cm). This species, found somewhat commonly in the waters of Janao Bay, Anilao, may be a subspecies or separate species related to *Wunderpus photogenicus.*

Tonguefish
Species unknown

This 1 inch (2.5 cm) juvenile tonguefish was found 65 feet (nearly 20 m) beneath the surface in a part of Janao Bay over 500 feet (150 m) deep. It came up to feed in the upper waters perhaps one last time as it now looks ready to settle on the bottom in a matter of days.

Eel
Species unknown

It's night in Balayan
Bay, Anilao. This larval
eel in the Leptocephalus
stage curls up into a tight
circle like a cobra, presumably adopting this pose as a
strategy to confuse predators and
to avoid looking like a protein-rich fish.
The eel's transparent body makes it even
less noticeable. Eel larvae, with their distinctive
shape, were described in the past as species in the genus
Leptocephalus. That name is no longer used as a genus,
but instead is applied as the common name for eel larvae.

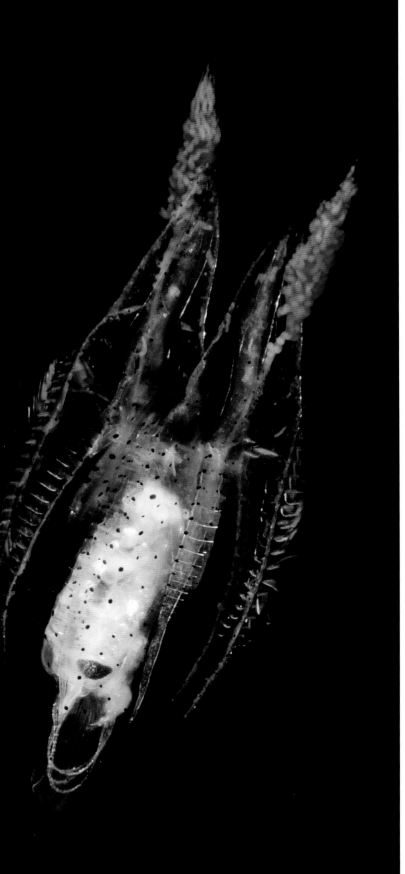

CHAPTER 4

The Gulf Stream Procession of Life

Linda Ianniello and Susan Mears were already dedicated divers and macro photographers when they heard that a local South Florida company, Pura Vida Divers, was going to offer blackwater diving. Both have been hooked ever since, Linda with 330 blackwater dives and Susan with more than 100 and counting.

On a typical night, their dive boat leaves Lake Worth Inlet in southeast Florida at about 7:30 PM heading five or six miles (8–10 km) south and then straight out six miles (10 km) offshore to the edge of the Gulf Stream. The bottom there is about 700 to 750 feet (213–229 m) below the surface — which has proved to be a good spot for vertically migrating fish larvae.

Susan describes the dive: "Entering the water, we will drift for up to 10 miles (16 km) north, depending on the strength of the current on a given night. We generally start the dive at a depth of about 50 feet (15 m) and work our way up to about 20 feet (6 m). Ideally, after the dive, we end the night out of the water opposite the inlet for a straight and quick run back in. It's then about 11 PM or midnight. By the time we've got home and cleaned the salt water off our cameras and had a look at the photos, it can be 3 AM."

The famous Gulf Stream is a river of life — a massive, 56-mile (90 km) wide, warm surface current that flows north along the coast of Florida at an average speed of 4 mph (6.4 kph) before heading northeast off North Carolina. Part of it heads toward far northwestern Europe while another part of the current crosses to West Africa before circling back clockwise as part of the North Atlantic

« **Hyperiid amphipod inside a ctenophore or comb jelly**

subtropical gyre. The Gulf Stream transports nearly 4 billion cubic feet (113 million m³) of water per second — an amount greater than the water carried by all the world's rivers combined. Riding that river are innumerable fish and invertebrate larvae, an entire world of plankton, as well as larger fishes, cephalopods, even whales.

As with other blackwater photographers, Linda and Susan face the challenge of identifying the species of plankton they find. The Blackwater Photo Group on Facebook has made it fun to post photos and find out what's what. More and more scientists are keen to see and identify the images, so they've joined the group, too.

Linda's and Susan's best finds in the Gulf Stream to date include a pelagic nudibranch, or sea slug (one of Linda's passions), a sea butterfly with the two appendages looking like green tree leaves and a female paper nautilus, a fairly rare deep-sea octopus that pulled Linda down to a depth of 100 feet (30 m) as she tried to photograph it. Susan likes to photograph everything from rare fish larvae to worms and gelatinous zooplankton. Her favorite find in the Gulf Stream was a beautiful and rare deep-sea snaketooth swallower, which she was amazed to bump into at the end of a dive in only 15–20 feet (4.6–6 m) of water. Says Susan, "This is a deepsea fish, but you don't have to dive deep to find its amazing larvae; you just have to be lucky." In recent years, Linda and Susan have noticed that larval billfish, such as marlin and sailfish, are turning up, especially around September.

"The diving itself is easy," says Susan. "You're just floating along. The hard part for us is that we are the guides for ourselves and need to find the creatures and then try to focus on an often-transparent subject that is tiny and constantly moving in the dark. Blackwater photography is extremely difficult; it takes patience and practice."

"Some animals avoid the lights and will react either by spinning or heading for the shallows or deep water," says Linda. "Our chances of taking photographs often improve if we turn the focus lights to the red option. The red light is tolerated more by some of the fish larvae."

"My focus has always been on getting a good ID-type image, and I make my images available to scientists," Linda adds. Recently, Linda and Susan have decided to help collect a few samples for the scientists researching larval evolution and behavior. "I used to be opposed to collecting these creatures," says Susan, "but now I've changed my mind if they are used to further science and identification."

"I feel that I owe the Smithsonian and other scientists for all their help with identifying my images, as long as I know the samples we collect will not sit on a shelf for years but will be of use," adds Linda. "But I have found it quite difficult and time-consuming to collect a moving subject in the dark while hanging on to a large camera set-up in the middle of the water column."

"Almost everything we see is very small, an inch or less," Linda continues. "But occasionally something big comes around. Swordfish are known to be aggressive and over six years, we have seen maybe two adults come close. Everyone worries about sharks, but they are rare and don't hang around. Occasionally, we get a silky shark that is inquisitive, but not aggressive. The big fish hear our bubbles and generally stay away from these noisy, clumsy intruders."

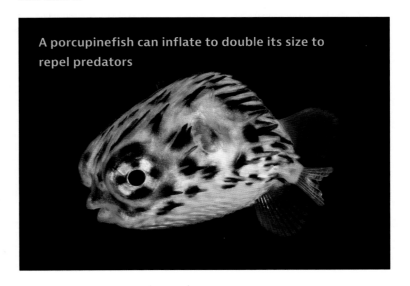

A porcupinefish can inflate to double its size to repel predators

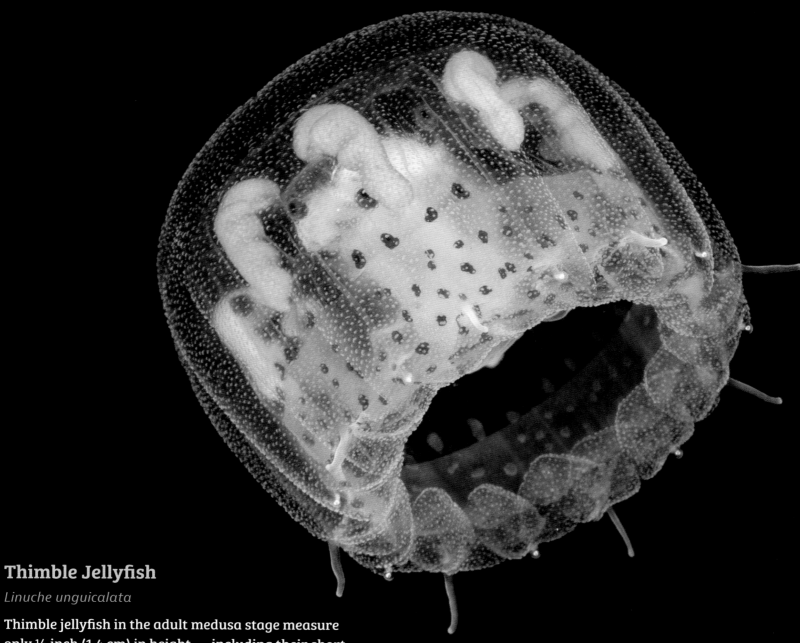

Thimble Jellyfish
Linuche unguicalata

Thimble jellyfish in the adult medusa stage measure only ½ inch (1.4 cm) in height — including their short tentacles. Also called sea thimbles, they live in the Gulf of Mexico, Caribbean and adjacent North Atlantic, ranging from the surface all the way down to 16,400 feet (5,000 m). Thimble jellyfish larvae are largely responsible for the itchy condition called seabather's eruption, which occurs when the stinging nematocysts that they use to defend themselves are fired into human skin.

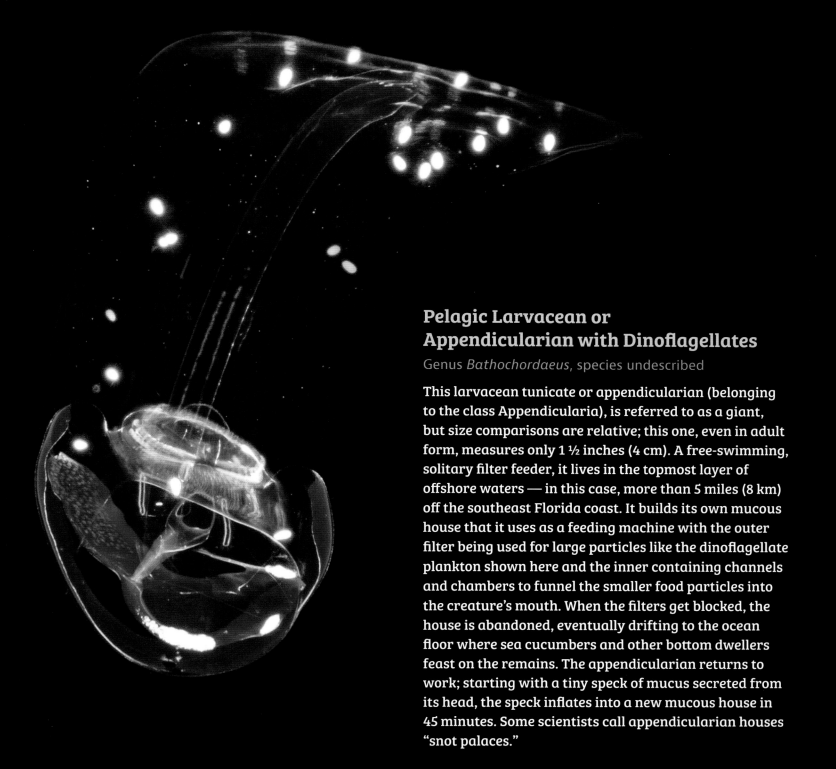

Pelagic Larvacean or Appendicularian with Dinoflagellates

Genus *Bathochordaeus*, species undescribed

This larvacean tunicate or appendicularian (belonging to the class Appendicularia), is referred to as a giant, but size comparisons are relative; this one, even in adult form, measures only 1 ½ inches (4 cm). A free-swimming, solitary filter feeder, it lives in the topmost layer of offshore waters — in this case, more than 5 miles (8 km) off the southeast Florida coast. It builds its own mucous house that it uses as a feeding machine with the outer filter being used for large particles like the dinoflagellate plankton shown here and the inner containing channels and chambers to funnel the smaller food particles into the creature's mouth. When the filters get blocked, the house is abandoned, eventually drifting to the ocean floor where sea cucumbers and other bottom dwellers feast on the remains. The appendicularian returns to work; starting with a tiny speck of mucus secreted from its head, the speck inflates into a new mucous house in 45 minutes. Some scientists call appendicularian houses "snot palaces."

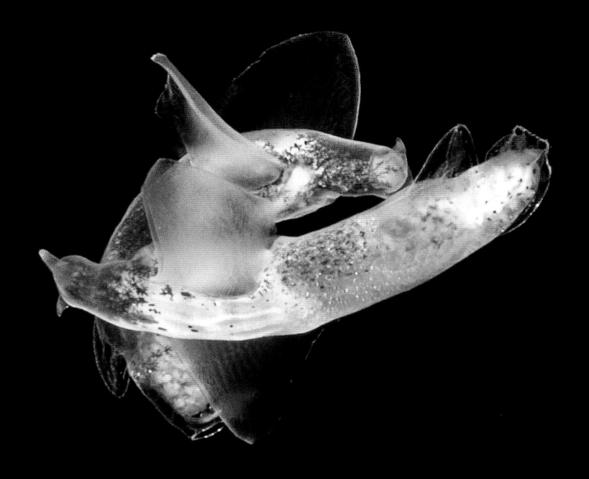

Sea Angels
Pneumoderma violaceum

Sea angels are gastropod mollusks, also known as sea slugs. These two males, ¾ inch long (2 cm), are mating in the waters at the edge of the Gulf Stream off Florida. As they hug, they spin rapidly around. Both males then store sperm until they grow and eventually change to become females. Then they lay eggs and use the stored sperm to fertilize them. The eggs hatch into larvae within a few days.

Ctenophore, or Comb Jelly (right)
Haeckelia rubra

This rare tropical and subtropical ctenophore was encountered in the surface waters of southeast Florida where the bottom is 500 to 700 feet (150–220 m) below the surface. Along with the attractive pulsing colors of this ¾ inch long (2 cm) adult are stinging nematocysts in its tentacles. Most ctenophores do not have nematocysts. Research has shown that this species avoids most other hydromedusae and siphonophores but will readily eat the tentacles of the medusa *Aegina citrea*, which has similar nematocysts. The researchers suggest that *Haeckelia rubra* may be incorporating the medusa's stinging cells into its own body for protection.

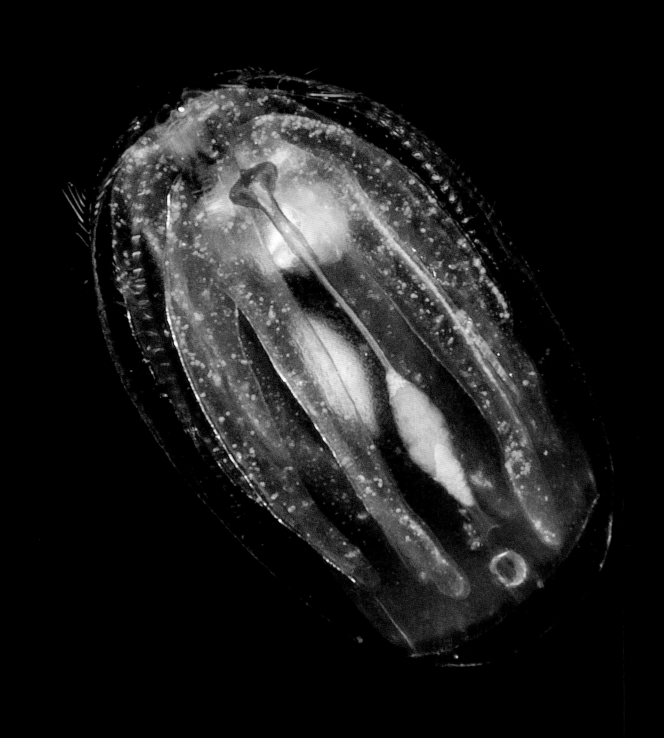

Porcupinefish

Genus *Diodon*, species unknown,
possibly *Diodon holocanthus*

Dolphins, tuna and zebra mantis shrimp eat juvenile porcupinefish like this 1 inch (2.5 cm) big-eyed individual. Some species of adult porcupinefish, also known as balloonfish, are poisonous, with ovaries and a liver containing tetrodotoxin, a neurotoxin 1,200 times more potent than cyanide. This poison, plus their ability to inflate to twice their normal size, gives them protection from most potential predators. On Charles Darwin's five-year journey on the *Beagle*, he encountered porcupinefish, noting that they swim upside down when inflated.

Hydromedusa (right)

Turritopsis nutricula

This adult hydromedusa has a bell of up to ½ inch (1.3 cm), although it can be much smaller. It is found in the Caribbean and Gulf Stream off Florida and was once thought to be the immortal jellyfish, able to transform itself by returning to the juvenile polyp stage in an endless cycle. The only way it could die is if it got swallowed by fish or blended by a boat propellor. More recent studies have confirmed that the true immortal jellyfish is its family member *Turritopsis dohrnii*, known to live in the Mediterranean and may have circumglobal distribution. Further studies await *T. nutricula* to determine if it has some of the special qualities of its now famous close relative.

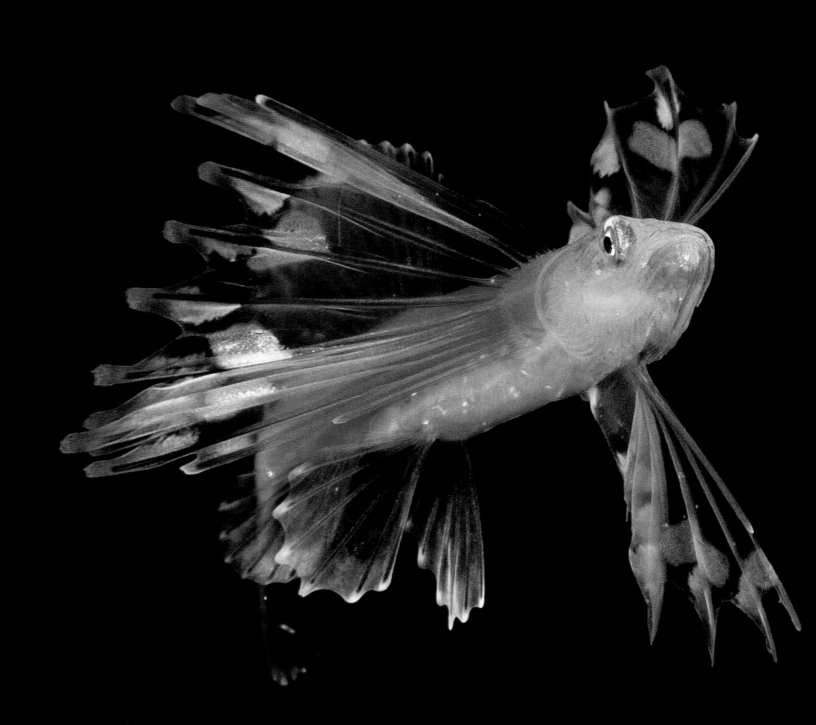

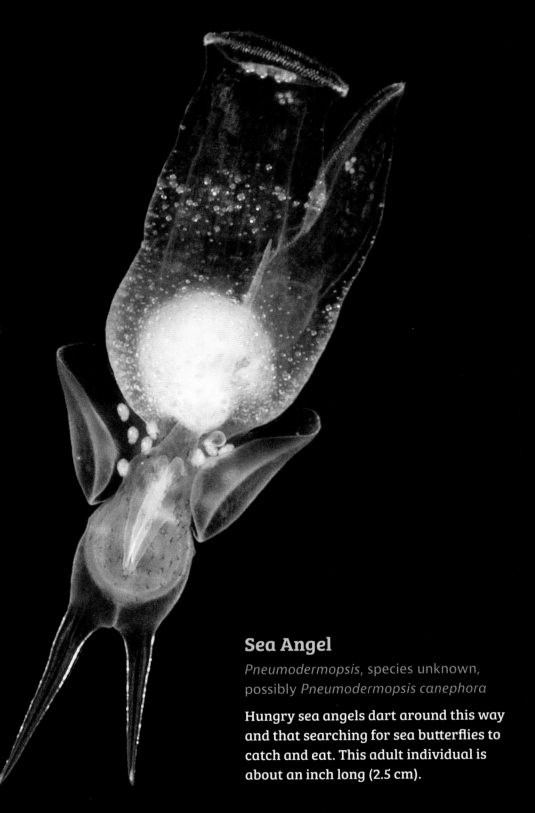

Tripodfish (left)

Genus Bathypterois, species unknown

Also known as spiderfishes, the little known and rarely seen tripodfishes in their adult form stay down on the bottom from 3,280 to 20,000 feet (1,000–6,000 m) below the surface. They use two of their pelvic-fin and one of their caudal-fin rays, that in one species can be up to 3.2 feet long (1 m), to prop themselves up like a tripod. Like most deep-sea living fishes, they have large mouths and small eyes. Shown here is a larval tripodfish about ¾ inch long (2 cm), which feeds in the surface waters of the Gulf Stream at night.

Sea Angel

Pneumodermopsis, species unknown, possibly Pneumodermopsis canephora

Hungry sea angels dart around this way and that searching for sea butterflies to catch and eat. This adult individual is about an inch long (2.5 cm).

87

Ctenophore or Comb Jelly and Hyperiid Amphipod

Genus *Callianira*, species unknown

About an inch long (2.5 cm), this adult *Callianira* cteno-phore is from the phylum of marine invertebrates called comb jellies. Like other comb jellies, this ctenophore has rows of comb-like plates with cilia that beat to help them swim. As they swim, the combs diffract light to create pulsing colors, adding to their bioluminescent display. Ctenophores are said to be voracious; has it just eaten a hyperiid amphipod half its size? More likely this is a parasitic hyperiid living inside the ctenophore and presenting a serious problem. The tentacles in this ctenophore, the pink curls, are normally extended for feeding but here they are withdrawn.

Hydromedusa

Cytaeis tetrastyla

This hydromedusa is found mainly in tropical and subtropical waters of the global open ocean. It lives in the water column down to 700 feet (210 m) but comes up near the surface to feed at night. This adult individual has a bell less than ¼ inch (0.5 cm) across. It was found 5 miles (8 km) off the coast of Florida near the western edge of the Gulf Stream.

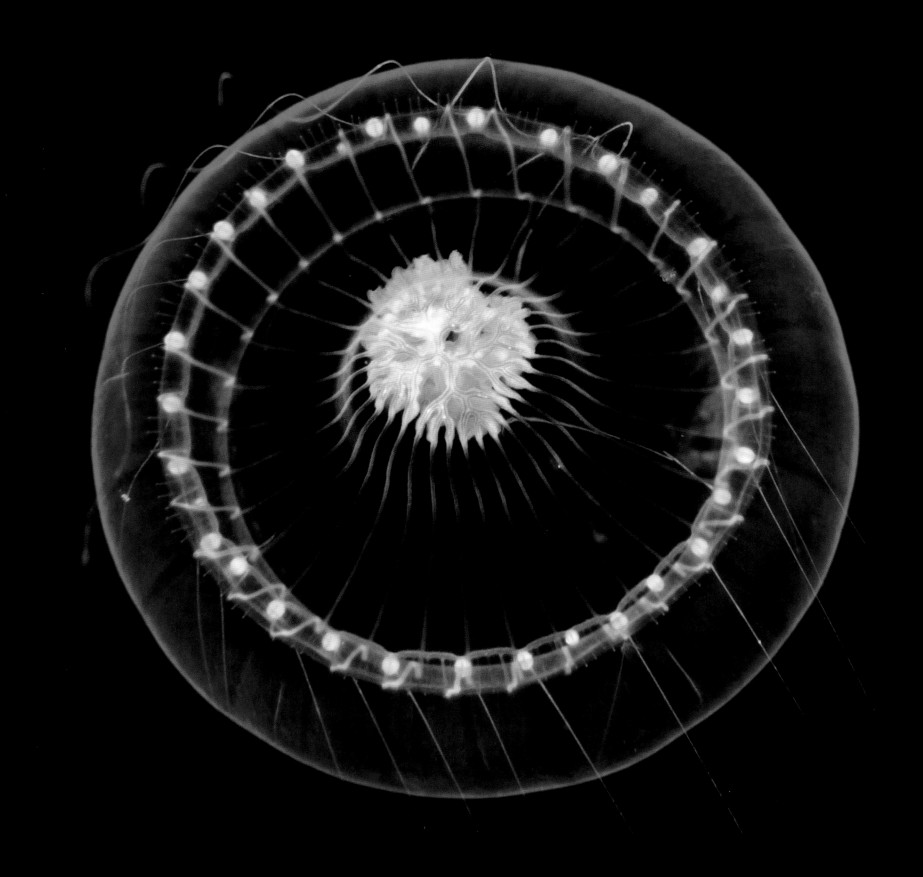

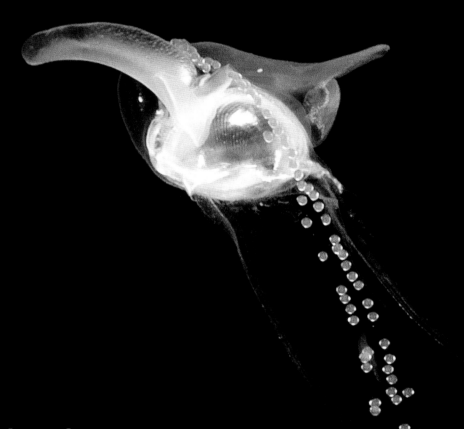

Sea Butterfly
Diacavolinia longirostris

Sea butterflies are a type of sea snail, also called pteropods, so named because they appear to be flying when they use their wing-like flaps to swim. Some 5 miles (8 km) off southeast Florida at the western edge of the Gulf Stream, a sea butterfly spawns, producing its uniquely shaped eggs. This adult measures about ½ inch long (1.3 cm).

Hydromedusa (left)
Orchistoma pileus

Most of the more than 800 species of hydromedusae in the world ocean are less than ⅜ inch (1 cm) and transparent, rarely noticed even by divers. This adult individual is large by comparison — 1 ½ inches (3.8 cm) across. Resident to the western North Atlantic, especially the Caribbean and Gulf Stream, this species ranges to a depth of nearly 6,000 feet (1,800 m). Like other hydromedusae, it is carnivorous, using its nematocysts, or stinging cells, to capture its largely planktonic prey. The source of the green coloring is unknown but could come from bacteria.

Cusk Eel (right)

Brotulotaenia, species unknown

In its larval form, this elongate bony fish measures only an inch long (2.5 cm). It displays flamboyant appendages that may make other hungry fish avoid it because the fins look like they're carrying the nematocyst stinging capsules found on the tentacles of siphonophores. As it matures, the larval cusk eel loses its appendages and moves to deeper water near the sea bottom.

Whitenose Pipefish

Cosmocampus albirostris

This juvenile whitenose pipefish, 3 inches long (7.6 cm), appeared one night at the edge of the Gulf Stream. The species is commonly found on reefs in the tropical and subtropical Atlantic, ranging down to about 165 feet (50 m) depth. As an adult, it can grow up to 8 inches long (20 cm). The male of this species carries the eggs in a brood pouch found under the tail. Called a cryptic species, it can easily camouflage itself against the reef or other bottom waters when needed.

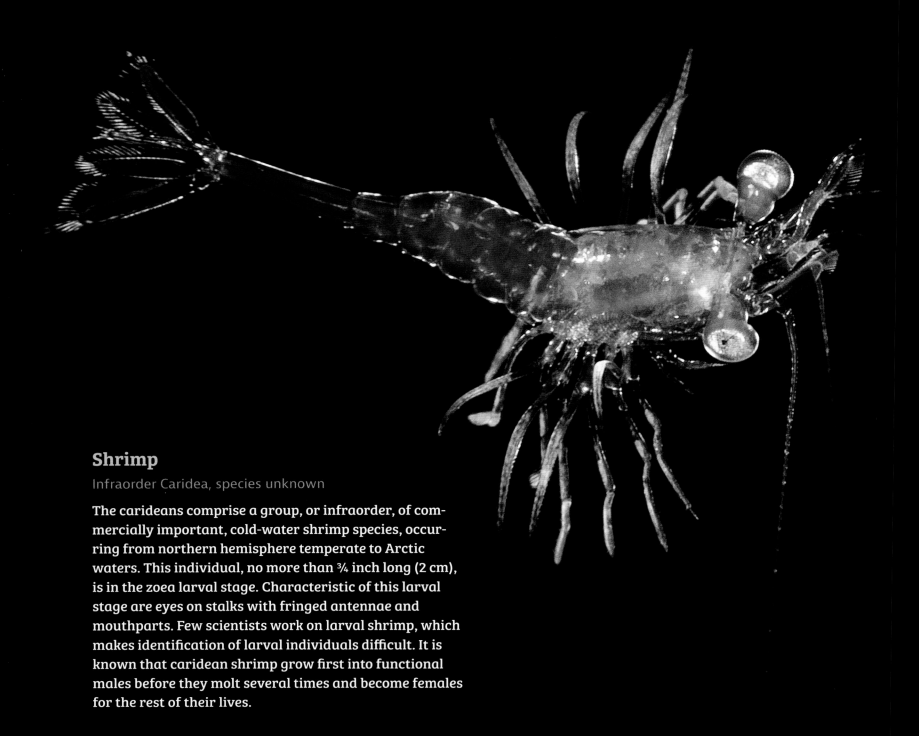

Shrimp

Infraorder Caridea, species unknown

The carideans comprise a group, or infraorder, of commercially important, cold-water shrimp species, occurring from northern hemisphere temperate to Arctic waters. This individual, no more than ¾ inch long (2 cm), is in the zoea larval stage. Characteristic of this larval stage are eyes on stalks with fringed antennae and mouthparts. Few scientists work on larval shrimp, which makes identification of larval individuals difficult. It is known that caridean shrimp grow first into functional males before they molt several times and become females for the rest of their lives.

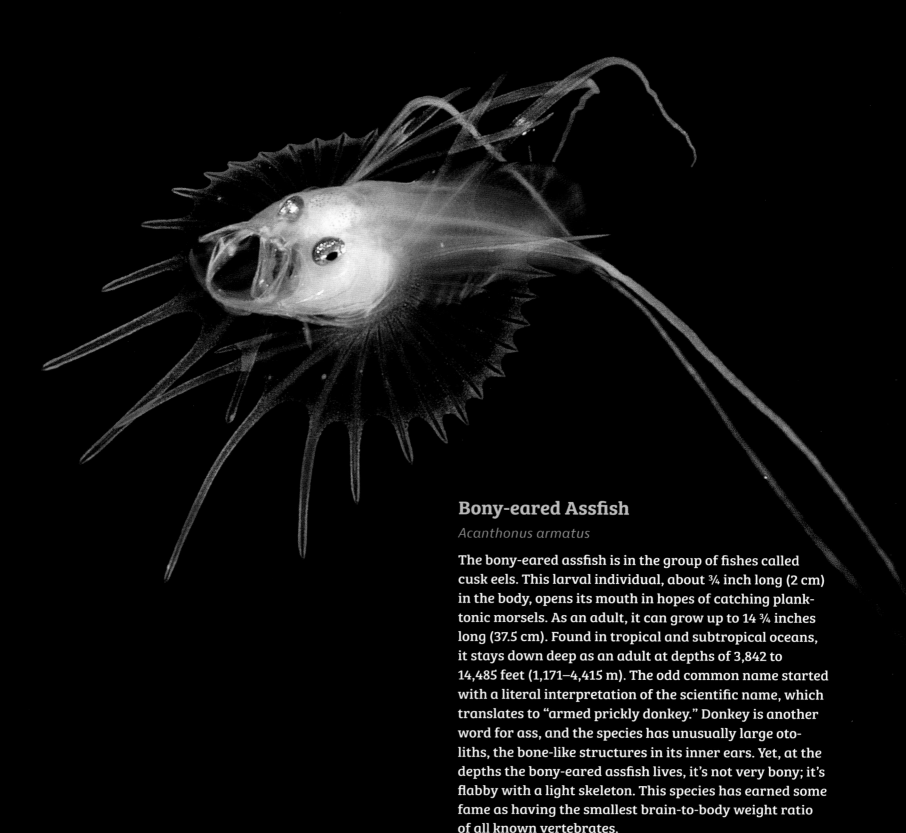

Bony-eared Assfish

Acanthonus armatus

The bony-eared assfish is in the group of fishes called
cusk eels. This larval individual, about ¾ inch long (2 cm)
in the body, opens its mouth in hopes of catching planktonic morsels. As an adult, it can grow up to 14 ¾ inches
long (37.5 cm). Found in tropical and subtropical oceans,
it stays down deep as an adult at depths of 3,842 to
14,485 feet (1,171–4,415 m). The odd common name started
with a literal interpretation of the scientific name, which
translates to "armed prickly donkey." Donkey is another
word for ass, and the species has unusually large oto-
liths, the bone-like structures in its inner ears. Yet, at the
depths the bony-eared assfish lives, it's not very bony; it's
flabby with a light skeleton. This species has earned some
fame as having the smallest brain-to-body weight ratio
of all known vertebrates.

Polychaete Worm

Tribe Alciopini, species unknown

This tribe of worms, exact species unknown, is called Alciopini. It's a polychaete, or segmented worm, a carnivorous animal that lives its entire life in the water column as plankton. It has big glowing eyes characteristic of this family. This 1 inch long (2.5 cm) adult lives at the edge of the Gulf Stream off Florida. In other parts of the world, they will circle around balls of eggs, not eating them. They are thought to be the worm's own eggs.

Narcomedusae Jellyfish and Amphipod

Pegantha polystriata and Order Amphipoda,
species unknown

Floating in the surface waters at the western edge of the
Gulf Stream, this adult hydromedusan jellyfish, named
in 2021 as *Pegantha polystriata* with help from Linda
Ianniello's photographs, is only ½ inch (1.3 cm) wide. On
this night, it has an amphipod visitor — probably not
prey. Linda often sees hdromedusae with one or more
crustaceans in the bell, and they don't appear to be
trapped or in distress.

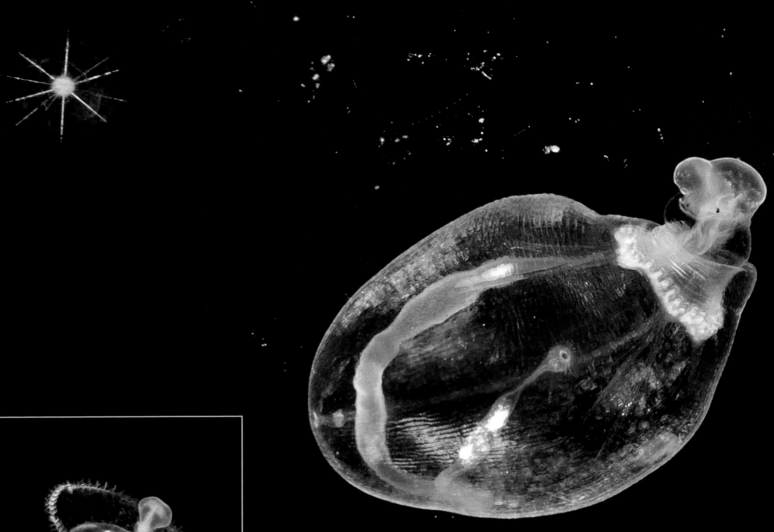

Peanut Worm

Phylum Sipuncula, species unknown

The planktonic larval stage of peanut worms is referred to as a pelagosphaera larva. These unsegmented marine worms are sometimes referred to as star worms. This individual is ½ inch long (1.3 cm). When it becomes an adult, it will settle on the bottom.

Tube Anemone
Subclass Ceriantharia, species unknown

Ceriantharians, or tube-dwelling anemones, float through the open ocean surface waters waving their sinuous arms in the first part of their life. This larval tube anemone has a body less than ½ inch (1.3 cm) across. It was photographed off Florida, near the Gulf Stream. As an adult, it will retire to a solitary existence, burying itself in soft sediments on the bottom, mainly in shallow seas.

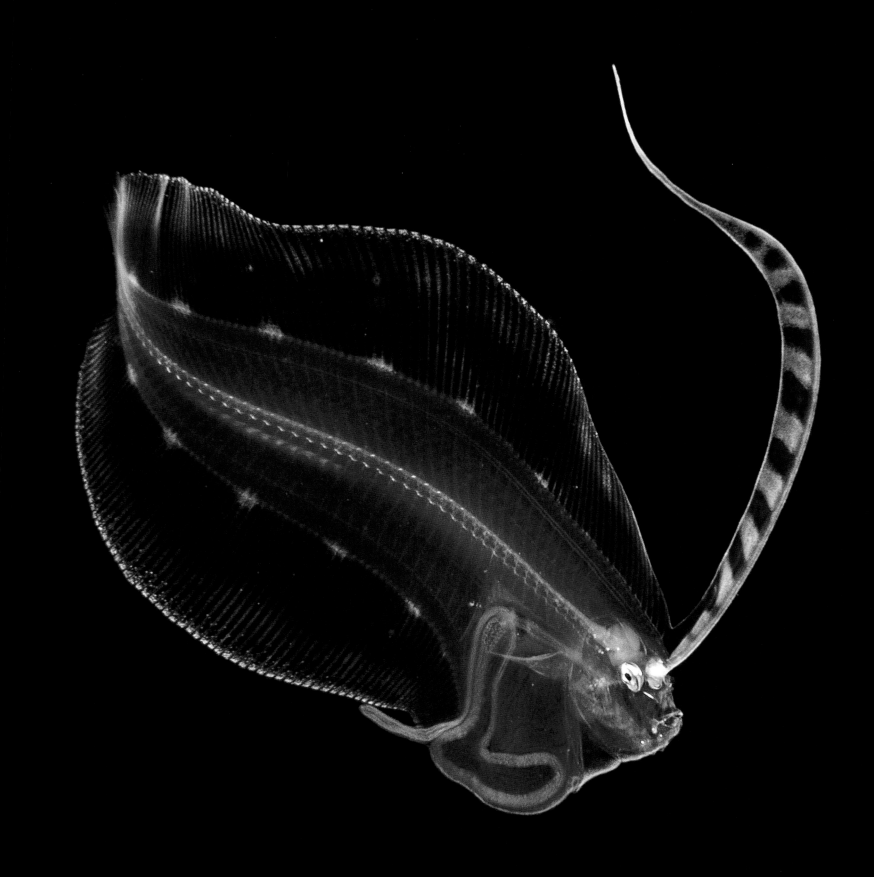

Deepwater Flounder (left)

Monolene sessilicauda

This larval deepwater flounder drifts through near-surface waters at night, gobbling up plankton. As an inch long (2.5 cm) larva, it relies on transparency and a fin ray that may mimic a siphonophore or jellyfish tentacle to confuse predators. This one was found off southeast Florida, but this western Atlantic species can be seen anywhere along the coast of the United States through tropical waters to as far south as Brazil. Once mature, measuring up to about 7 inches (18 cm), deepwater flounder retire to a shell or muddy bottom from 250 to 3,400 feet (80–1,040 m) below the surface, both its eyes looking up from the left side.

Pelagic Amphipod, with young

Phronimella elongata

This adult amphipod has no common name. Here, a female amphipod lives with her young in a kind of barrel made of gelatinous zooplankton. This female was found near the Gulf Stream in surface waters at night, but later it will move into the mesopelagic ocean, typically 1,000 to 2,000 feet (300–600 m) in depth.

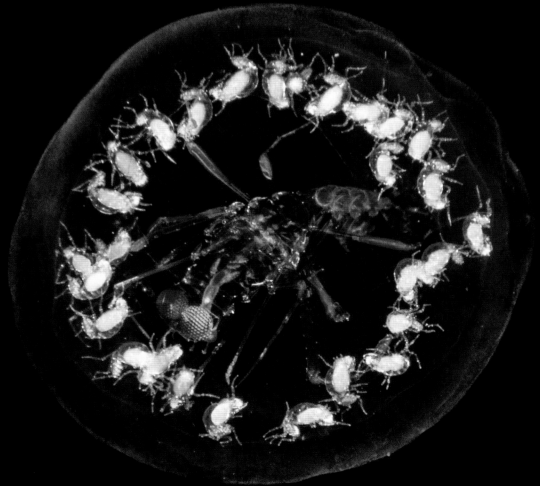

Sargassum Swimming Crab and probable Jack

Portunus sayi and Jack, species unknown

This 1 inch long (2.5 cm) Sargassum swimming crab is a presumed juvenile nearing adulthood. It drifts on the surface with the sargassum, dropping down into the water column to hunt. Resident to the western Atlantic Ocean and the Caribbean, it is typically found among the vast floating mats of Sargassum seaweed. This individual has been photographed at night in the act of catching a small fish, probably a jack.

Hydromedusa with Jacks (right)

Genus *Aequorea*, and Jacks, species unknown

This *Aequorea* hydromedusa is common to southeast Florida along the western edge of the Gulf Stream. The size of its umbrella-shaped bell is 1 ½ to 2 inches (3.8–5 cm) and the juvenile jacks are less than half an inch long (1.3 cm). The jacks often shelter inside the bell for protection. In some *Aequorea* species, the dome reaches 12 to 16 inches (30–40 cm) in diameter.

Pram Bug with Salp (right)

Genus *Phronima* and Family Salpidae, species unknown

A parasitic female pram bug, only ¼ inch long (0.6 cm), has invaded a salp, a kind of tunicate — sometimes called a sea grape. The pram bug, or hyperiid amphipod, has eaten the salp from the inside and laid tiny eggs. The female then rides along inside the empty salp shell, using it like a pram or buggy, taking care of her young. The killing and hijacking of the salp stands in contrast to the devoted motherly care for the pram bug's offspring. These dramas take place far from land in the open ocean, in this case at the edge of the Gulf Stream off southwest Florida.

Soapfish

Genus *Rypticus*, species unknown

Soapfishes are creatures of the night, both as young and adults, found in tropical and warm temperate Atlantic and eastern Pacific Ocean waters. This larval ¾ inch (2 cm) soapfish was found at the edge of the Gulf Stream off Florida. Soapfish larvae have evolved characteristics common to many larval fish — flared pectoral fins and transparency, plus a long filamentous dorsal-fin ray. Once their larval lives are complete, soapfishes move into relatively shallow reefs. Soapfishes, when stressed, are known to secrete toxic mucus from their skin that repels predators.

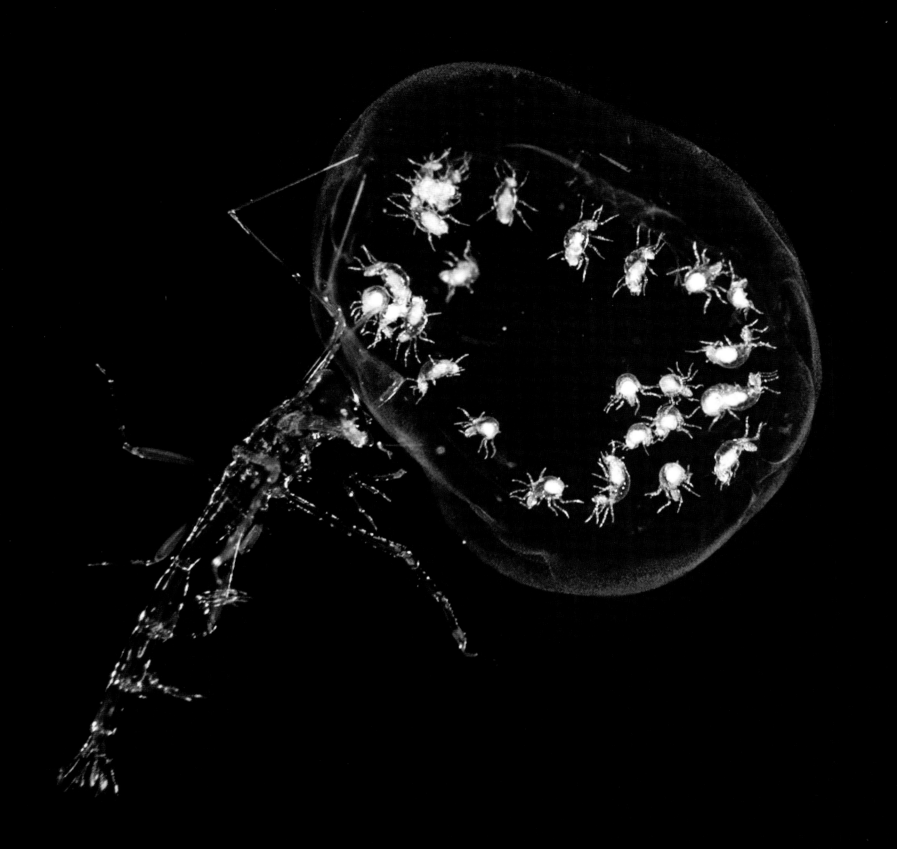

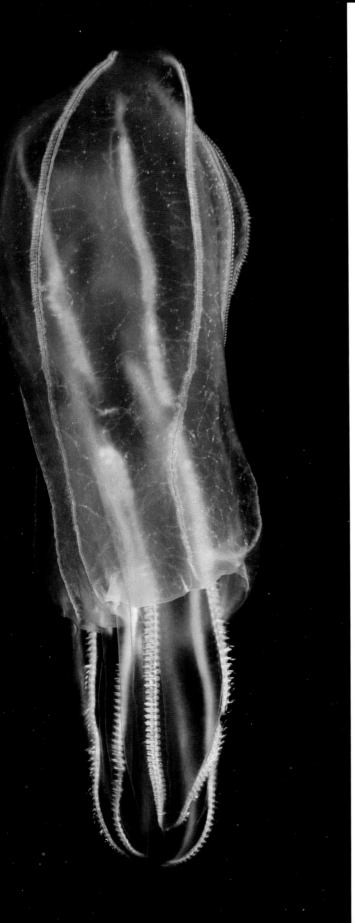

CHAPTER 5
Blackwater White Sea

The White Sea straddles the Arctic Circle in far north-western Russia. It's much closer to Finland, about 150 miles (250 km) to the west, than to Moscow, 1,000 miles (1,600 km) south. From October to April, the White Sea is indeed largely white as it is covered in ice and snow. In the summer, it is white, too. With up to 24 hours of daylight, the water's surface reflects the Arctic sky and sparkles white from the silicon and silicates carried by the massive freshwater rivers flowing into the White Sea. Despite all this whiteness, the underwater world down below can be as black as the mid-winter Arctic night.

Diver-photographer Alexander Semenov lives and works with other biologists as part of the group Aquatilis, dedicated to diving in these cold waters. Based at the White Sea Biological Station of Moscow State University, Alex is a skilled, passionate photographer of sea squirts, sea butterflies and other characteristic cold-water residents that are part of the marine riches of Velikaja Salma (Great Strait) Bay in the White Sea.

"We have strong currents here and we're tied to a tidal schedule to catch 40 to 70 minutes of still water," says Alex. "Until February, the ice is usually not thick enough, and it is risky to go far out on the ice on snowmobiles, so for safety reasons we don't dive during the polar winter."

"We start diving at the end of February or early March," says Alex. "As long as the ice is solid, we saw out the sinkholes and dive on the ropes, and when the ice breaks up and the currents start carrying huge ice floes across the strait, we drop the boat and maneuver between them, diving where we can."

« One comb jelly eats another comb jelly

"Sometimes we manage to get crystal-clear water when plankton has not yet appeared in the sea and the ice has not broken and the wind has not stirred the water. From March onwards, as the sun starts to shine brightly, everything changes quite rapidly under the ice, the water becomes turbid with the presence of plankton, and animals appear in waves, and then in large numbers all at once.

"First comes the phytoplankton bloom clouding the water. Next the arrow worms and ctenophores followed by hydromedusae and crustacean larvae. Then sea angels and sea butterflies turn up. By June, the large, stinging, jelly-like scyphomedusae appear.

"Sometimes, during summer and even in autumn, certain animals that should not be in plankton during that season appear almost out of nowhere," says Alex, "or the current brings thousands of tiny newborn ctenophores. I still don't understand the full life cycle of many planktonic animals and how that links to different seasons of the year."

Some 700 known invertebrate species and 60 fish species inhabit the White Sea, which has a mean depth of only 200 feet (60 m) and a maximum depth of 1,115 feet (340 m). Alex says there are "not so many creatures vertically migrating in the White Sea because it's a relatively shallow water sea. The planktonic species are spread all over the water column."

Although remote from Moscow and other European cities, the 35,000 mile² (90,000 km²) White Sea is a busy traffic corridor connecting the ports of Murmansk and other Arctic cities as far away as Siberia to Saint Petersburg and the rest of Europe through the White Sea–Baltic Canal. However, the White Sea Biological Station and surrounding water opposite the biological station and the adjacent nature reserve remain comparatively remote, with no roads. Access to the isolated White Sea Biological Station is by boat in the summer and snowmobiles the rest of the year.

Across the Velikaja Salma Bay lies Veliky Island, the largest island of the Kandalaksha State Nature Reserve. One of the oldest nature reserves in Russia, created in 1932, it extends north to the Barents Sea and includes more than 550 islands with 74% of the 272 mile² (705 km²) site being marine. It is a strict nature reserve, open for scientists and by permit for environmental education.

Alex explains the appeal of blackwater diving: "For a marine biologist, it is like a huge book full of wonderful stories whose pages you can turn by diving into different seas and oceans and discovering new things. Every dive and deepwater exploration is like poking a haystack with the tiniest of needles — divers are the needles since they plunge into a vast globe of water teeming with life and bump into just a few of the inhabitants …. The average person has never heard of salps, siphonophores, comb jellies, appendicularians, ascidians and many others. My work aims to show a different world full of strange and wildly interesting things."

Sea angel hunting

Lion's Mane Jellyfish

Cyanea capillata

This young lion's mane jellyfish, only 2–2 ¾ inches (5–7 cm), has tentacles and mouth lobes just beginning to form. Even as young ephyra, it is an active, accomplished hunter. But in a few weeks of rapid development, it will grow into a monster with a dome eventually reaching 5 feet (1.5 m) across and tentacles 50 to 66 feet long (15–20 m).

INSET This less than ¼ inch (0.6 cm) lion's mane jellyfish is in the ephyra or larval stage with underdeveloped tentacles. It will eventually grow to be one of the largest jellyfish species in the world.

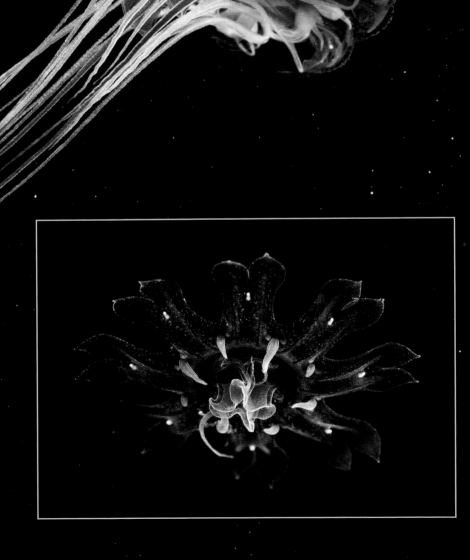

Big-eyed amphipod

Hyperia galba

This parasitic crustacean, ⅜ inch long (1 cm) with large green eyes, swims in search of its next host victim. Will it be jellyfish or comb jellies this time? When the amphipod finds a jellyfish, it eats its way into the tissues, settling often near the stomach or in the gonads. A pregnant female amphipod carrying a brood pouch of eggs turns the jellyfish into a floating nursery and canteen. In time, the amphipod family will devour the jellyfish host from the inside out. After the jellyfish dies, the big-eyed amphipods are then free to swim in the water column and search for a new host.

Arctic Comb Jelly

Mertensia ovum

The Arctic comb jelly, or sea nut, has long tentacles as well as smaller tentillae, which are like stinging nematocysts but instead of toxins, they emit adhesives to ensnare zooplankton prey. Favorite food? Copepods. When the sticky tentacles are outstretched, they can be several times the length of the main body. This comb jelly is less than 2 inches long (5 cm). It is bioluminescent in various colors, with the comb rows beating in sequence. These comb rows are chemical sense organs, like antennae.

Comb Jelly

Beroe cucumis

This young ctenophore, one of the comb jelly species described in 1780 by Danish missionary Otto Fabricius, measures no more than ¾ inch long (2 cm). Drifting through the White Sea, the transparent body offers a glimpse of its recent meal — another tiny ctenophore, species unknown.

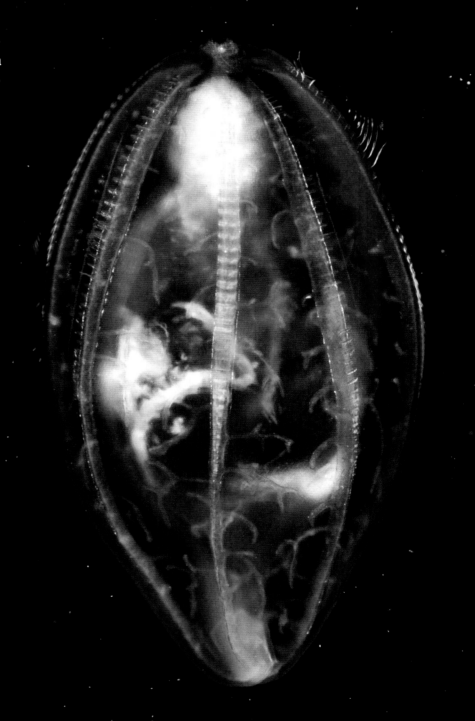

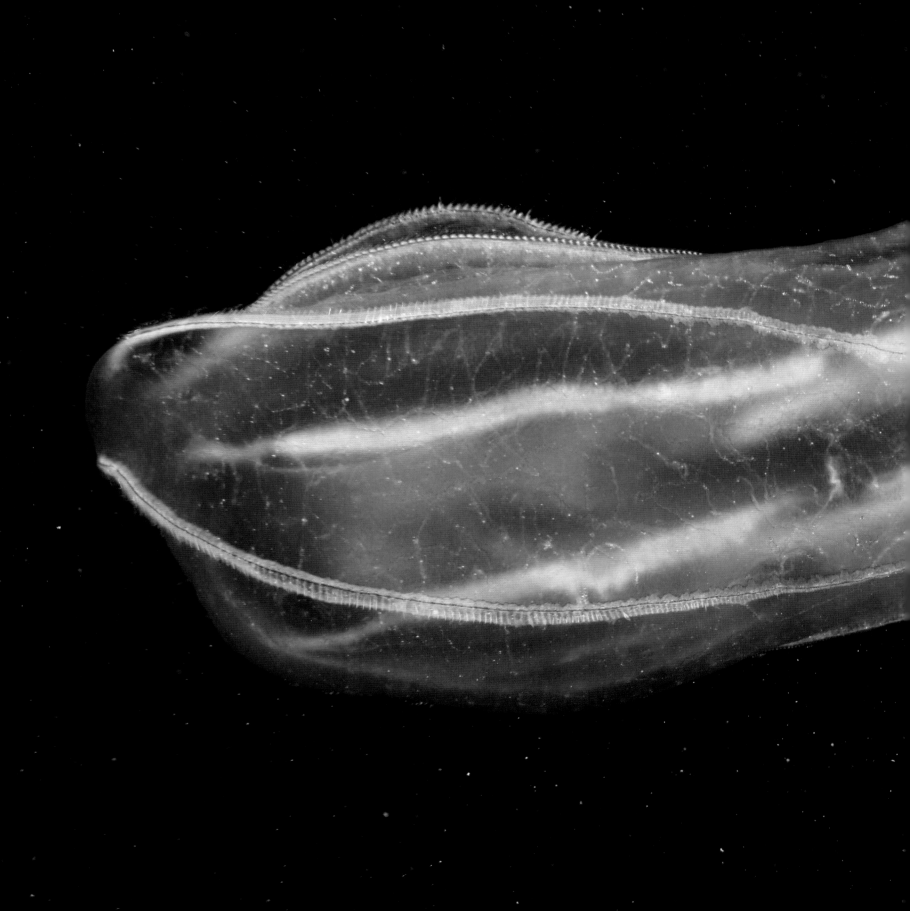

Comb Jelly swallowing probable Common Northern Comb Jelly

Beroe cucumis and probable *Bolinopsis infundibulum*

Beroe comb jellies are always on the hunt for other cteno-phores. Here, following a mouth-to-mouth confrontation 40 feet (12 m) down in the White Sea, a 4 inch long (10 cm) *Beroe* devours a similar size *Bolinopsis* ctenophore, using the tiny "teeth" of cilia at the edges of its mouth to grip its prey.

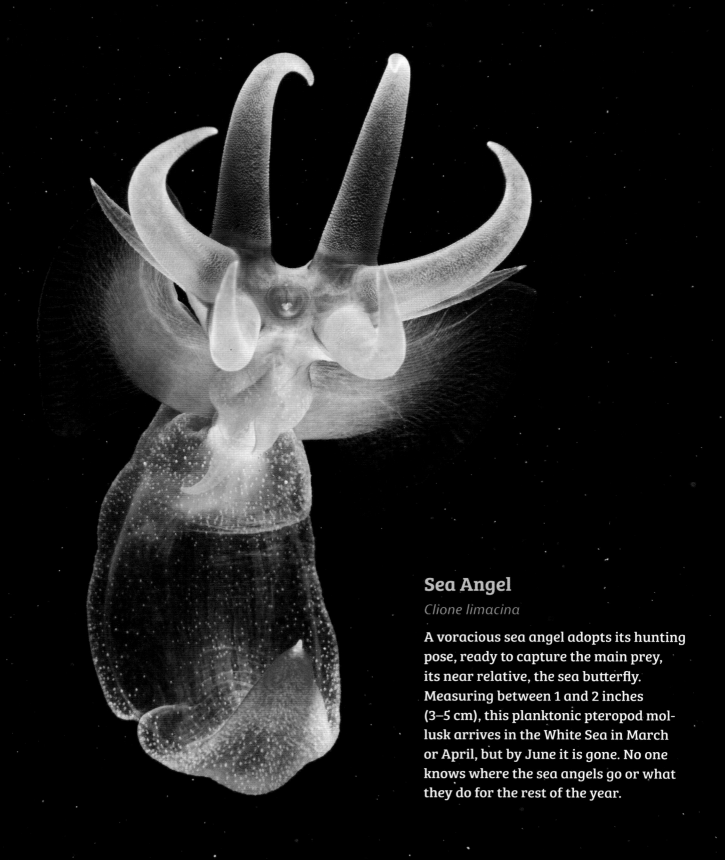

Sea Angel
Clione limacina

A voracious sea angel adopts its hunting pose, ready to capture the main prey, its near relative, the sea butterfly. Measuring between 1 and 2 inches (3–5 cm), this planktonic pteropod mollusk arrives in the White Sea in March or April, but by June it is gone. No one knows where the sea angels go or what they do for the rest of the year.

Comb Jelly feeding on Common Northern Comb Jelly

Beroe cucumis and *Bolinopsis infundibulum*

Swimming silently, mouth pursed tight, using its "lips" to detect potential prey, this *Beroe* comb jelly, close to 2 ¾ inches long (7 cm), has met its favorite food, another comb jelly. The *Beroe* uses its non-transparent red stomach to mask the glow of the bioluminescent common northern comb jelly that it has just eaten. This predator-prey drama normally occurs at depths of 1,300 to 6,540 feet (400–2,000 m), but it is happening here in the surface waters abuzz with plankton.

Starfish

Phylum Echinodermata, species unknown

Drifting through the White Sea just below surface, using its long outgrowths to paddle in the water column, this less than ⅛ inch long (0.3 cm) starfish larva grabs nutrients and tries to avoid being eaten. This is the last larval stage called brachiolaria larva. Note that the star is already forming at the base, a sign of almost reaching maturity.

Sea Leech eggs on a Sculptured Shrimp

Probable *Crangonobdella spitzbergensis* eggs on *Sclerocrangon boreas*

This is a close-up of eggs on the underside of a female sculptured shrimp, typically measuring up to about 1 ⁹/₁₆ inch (4 cm), although the record size is almost 6 inches long (14.5 cm). Note the yellow shrimp eggs and the tiny green parasitic leech eggs on the pleopods, the paired leg-like appendages that the shrimp uses for swimming as well as for carrying eggs.

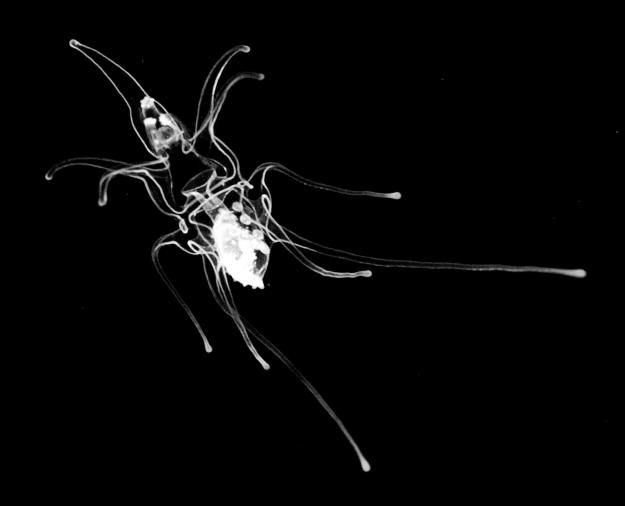

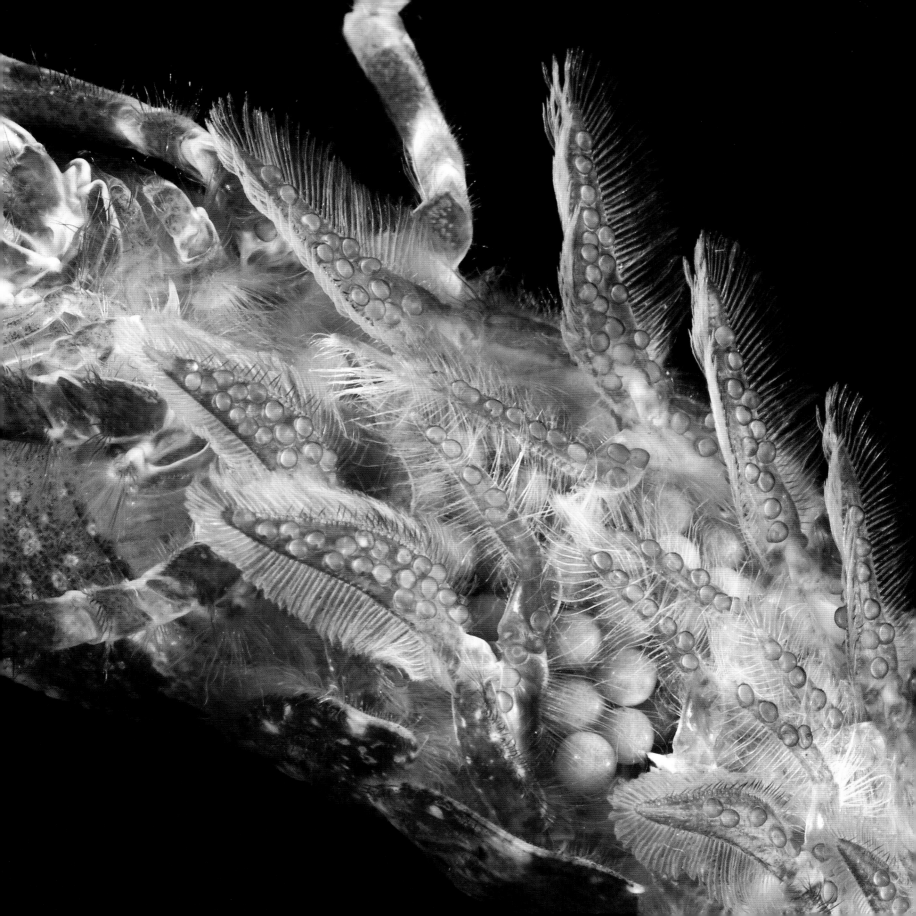

Parchment Tube Worm

Chaetopterus cautus

In Russian waters, north of the Sea of Japan/East Sea, this species of bristle worm, 3 to 4 inches long (8–10 cm), is one of 13,000 species of annelid worms that live in the ocean at all depths and are either nomadic or sedentary, attaching themselves to rocks or the sandy bottom. This one, looking like a cross between a yellow flower and a sea dragon, will construct a U-shape tube lined with mucus topped off with a chimney of parchment. The tube stays attached to the bottom and the worm never leaves the tube. Even though the tube obscures its beauty, the worm will sometimes glow brightly inside the tube, emitting a blue light. Despite considerable study, scientists are still puzzling over how and why this tube worm produces its bioluminescence.

Jellyfish with riding Sea Anemones (right)

Genera *Aequorea* and *Peachia*, species unknown

These larval sea anemones, from the Okhotsk Sea of Russia, also called actinia, range in size from ¼₀th to ¼ inch (.05 cm to 0.5 cm). When the larvae jump aboard *Aequorea* jellyfish, they have both a source of food and good protection wherever the jellyfish goes. As adults, the sea anemones detach from the jellyfish and settle on the bottom where they burrow into the sediment and turn into common burrowing creatures.

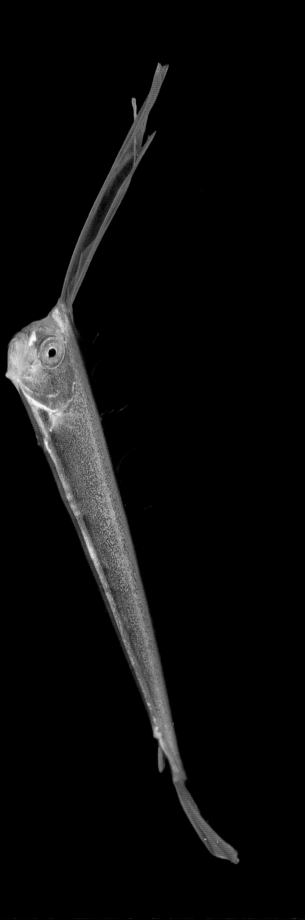

CHAPTER 6
The Precious Life of Plankton

Slipping into the water on a new moon night, Japanese diving photographer Ryo Minemizu can see the glowing snowy peak of Mount Fuji across the bay. Seconds later, he drops down into the middle of the dark planktonic world ready to meet the living objects of his desire.

"Why are the shapes and colors of plankton as small as a few millimeters so awe-inspiring?" asks Ryo. "It's because life is in its perfect state — drifting to the flow of the water in the natural environment."

That flow is the upwelling current driven in part by seasonal winds bringing up tiny creatures from the deepest part of the deepest bay in Japan — Suruga Bay off the Izu peninsula west of Tokyo. It is 8,200 feet (2,500 m) deep.

"These tiny creatures have dramatically transformed their appearance and behavior, taking note of the ecology of other creatures," says Ryo. "For plankton, it is the ability to live one's life, as much as possible, interconnected with others. The natural world is based on an exquisite balance, and the plankton are always trying to maintain that balance. I think that humans should live in nature without disturbing it, without putting a burden on it. Like the plankton, we should live in balance with the flow of nature."

Ryo started diving in Suruga Bay in 1990, after being invited on a dive by his senior manager. Inspired by the wonders of the underwater sea, Ryo quit his job and trained to become a diving instructor. When he discovered the pioneer blackwater photographs in Christopher Newbert's book *Within a Rainbowed Sea*, he determined

« Unicornfish swimming with its head held high

Larval octopus in the lights

to make the unravelling of the nighttime planktonic world his life's work. This would mean not only long hours in the water, up to eight hours a day, but constant experimentation with lenses, cameras and lighting to resolve the technical challenges of capturing life in the colors and resolution to reveal these mini-marvels as they are in nature.

Ryo needed to find the best methods for photographing plankton with lighting that would attract, or at least not discourage, his subjects. After much experimentation and new lighting developments the past two decades, he has settled on multiple RGBlue LED lights (1,500 lumen maximum) that are not the brightest available but that seem to agree with his living subjects and also provide the most natural as opposed to brighter, artificial light.

At the same time, he has evolved his own careful protocol for blackwater interaction with creatures:

» Change the diving location daily. Never go back to the same place on successive nights and leave at least seven days before returning to the same location.

» After two visits in successive weeks to the same place, wait eight weeks before the next visit.
» Restrict diving in one place to a total of seven days in a year.

Following these rules gives respect to these creatures, most of them young animals trying to make their way. It also reduces the chances of a predator fish habituating to an area from the presence of lights; the presence of predators alone can make vulnerable plankton scarce.

Patience and precise attention to details are part of Ryo's operating manual. He talks about the challenge of drifting with the plankton at night, shooting with fast shutter speeds, controlling the depth of field to fractions of millimeters, while paying attention not to disturb the water around his subjects.

With more than 28,000 dives in a little more 30 years, he clearly loves spending time uncovering plankton lives. "Plankton symbolize how precious life is by their tiny existence."

Forktail Blenny
Meiacanthus atrodorsalis

Thirty-three feet (10 m) down, near Kume Island off Japan's tropical Okinawa Island, this big-eyed larval individual, less than an inch long (2.3 cm), popped up inches from Ryo Minemizu's blackwater lights and camera. The bright coloring indicates a juvenile nearing maturity that may have already test-landed on the seabed once. However, until it finds a safe place to stay, it will keep moving and riding the tide every night. In this late juvenile stage before they complete their planktonic lives, forktail blennies will alternately drift and spend time investigating the seafloor.

INSET Side view of the forktail blenny.

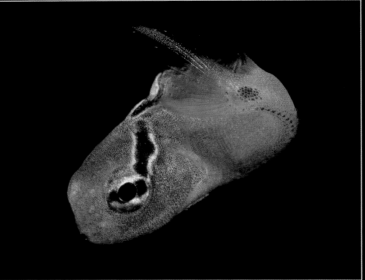

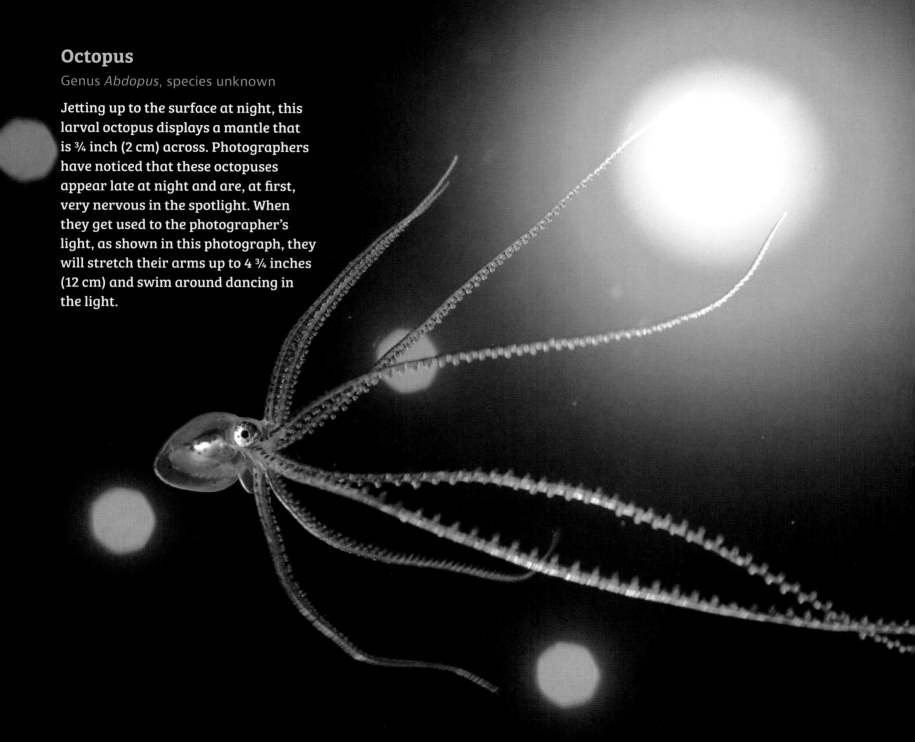

Octopus

Genus *Abdopus*, species unknown

Jetting up to the surface at night, this larval octopus displays a mantle that is ¾ inch (2 cm) across. Photographers have noticed that these octopuses appear late at night and are, at first, very nervous in the spotlight. When they get used to the photographer's light, as shown in this photograph, they will stretch their arms up to 4 ¾ inches (12 cm) and swim around dancing in the light.

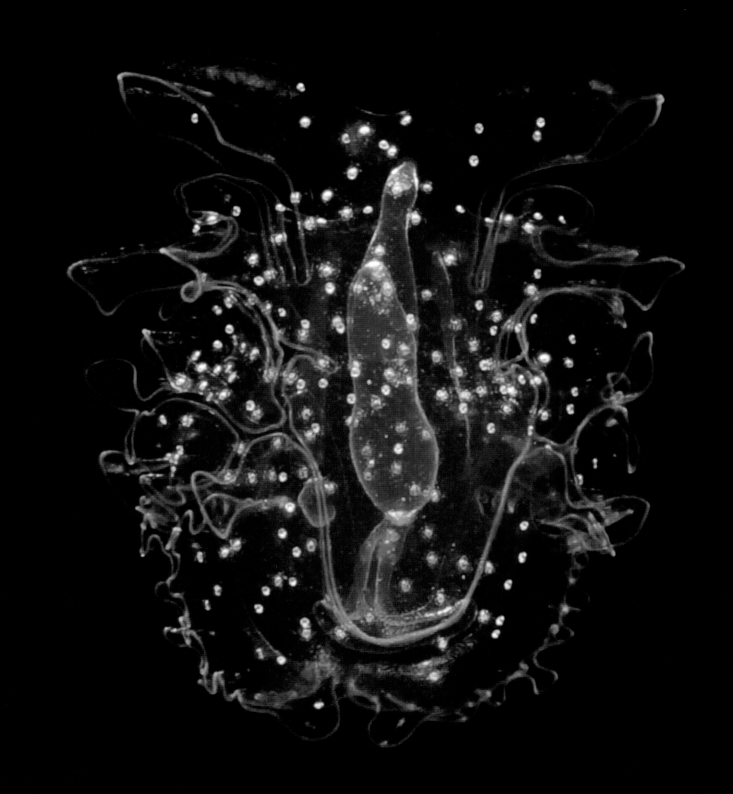

Sea Cucumber (left)

Species unknown

This less than ¼ inch (0.5 cm) mass of transparent, floating larvae is called auricularia. It's the first larval stage of a sea cucumber. The grains that look like bubbles scattered throughout are ossicles, tiny pieces of calcified material that become embedded in the body wall of sea cucumbers. After this floating auricularian larval stage, the prospective sea cucumber undergoes further changes in its metamorphosis. The next larval stages are called doliolaria and pentacula larva. The stage that follows those is the newly adult sea cucumber, which moves to the sea bottom to take up residence.

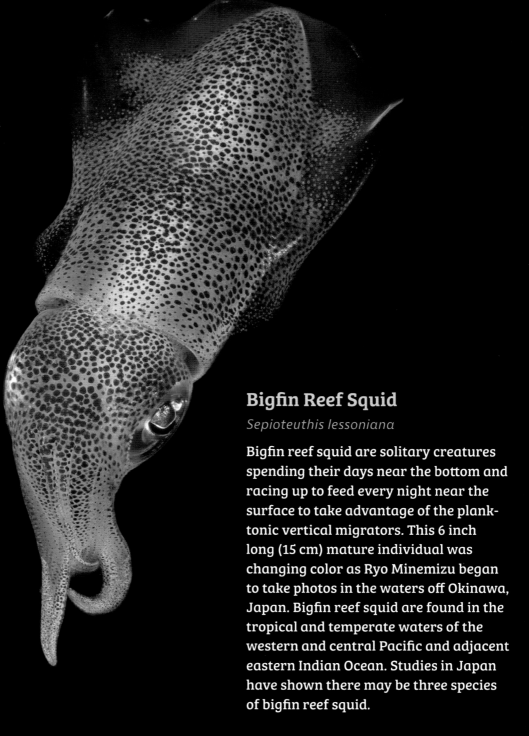

Bigfin Reef Squid

Sepioteuthis lessoniana

Bigfin reef squid are solitary creatures spending their days near the bottom and racing up to feed every night near the surface to take advantage of the planktonic vertical migrators. This 6 inch long (15 cm) mature individual was changing color as Ryo Minemizu began to take photos in the waters off Okinawa, Japan. Bigfin reef squid are found in the tropical and temperate waters of the western and central Pacific and adjacent eastern Indian Ocean. Studies in Japan have shown there may be three species of bigfin reef squid.

Broadclub Cuttlefish

Sepia latimanus

Broadclub cuttlefish live mainly in shallow waters and on coral reefs widely distributed along the coasts of the Indian and Pacific oceans. This ¾ inch (2 cm) juvenile can already change color and shape to look like coral or mangrove leaves. Divers remark on how peaceful and laid back they seem, with "gentle eyes." As adults, they grow to be the second largest of all cuttlefish, still gentle but with a mantle size of up to 20 inches (50 cm) and a weight exceeding 22 pounds (10 kg).

Bobtail Squid (right)

Species unknown

This juvenile bobtail squid, only ⅝ inches long (1.5 cm), may bury itself, typically in the sand, using camouflage to hide from predators. But as night approaches, the squid finds that the bioluminescent bacteria *Vibrio fischeri*, feeding on amino acid and sugar in the light organ of its body, have begun to glow. The color, pattern and intensity of the light may be shaped through pigment-containing groups of cells called chromatophores. The light may attract some prey and distract predators. The squid has a symbiotic relationship with the bioluminescent bacteria, which can benefit both species.

Harlequin Shrimp

Hymenocera picta

Only ¼ inch long (0.6 cm), this colorful shrimp is in the megalops larval stage. For now, it is transparent and covered in red pigment, which is less detectable by many predators than the colors that it will have as an adult. As it grows to maturity at about 2 inches long (5 cm), the shrimp has spots that become bigger and, if anything, gaudier, ranging in color from white to light pink with touches of red, orange, blue or purple. While the larva moves about in the water column, upon becoming an adult, the harlequin shrimp will stay on the sea bottom.

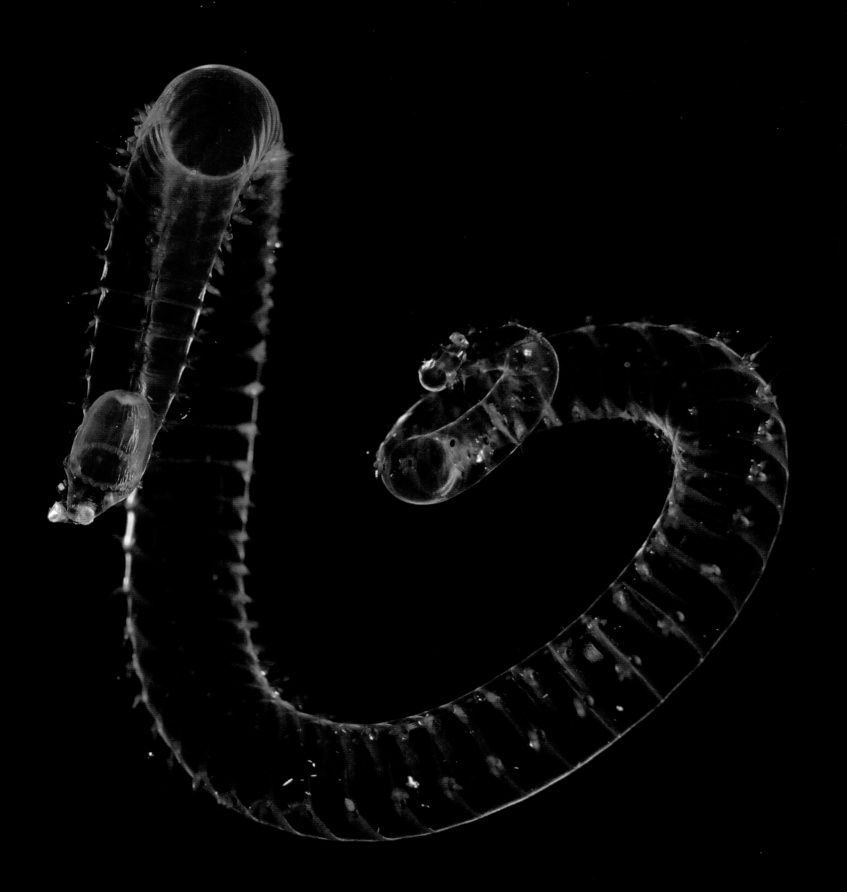

Polychaete Worm (left)

Family Phyllodocidae, species unknown

This red-eyed wonder, 2 ¾ inches long
(7 cm), is a mature transparent polychaete worm from the Alciopini tribe.
They sometimes coil themselves up
like a snake, which is assumed to be a
defensive pose.

Jellyfish and Lobster

Eutiara decorata and Family Scyllaridae,
species unknown

For the larval lobster in its phyllosoma
stage, boarding this fast-moving,
1 ¼ inch long (3 cm) transparent jellyfish
makes for a wild bronco ride. Usually,
phyllosomae choose much smaller species to ride on. This hydromedusa was
only recently described by scientists.

135

Tiger Sole

Genus *Soleichthy*, species unknown

Mimicry is at play in the shape and behavior of this ⅝ inch long (1.5 cm) larval tiger sole. As larva, the tiger sole looks like a poisonous flatworm and swims like one, too.

Unicornfish

Lophotus capellei

Rarely encountered, this larval fish, sometimes referred to as the North Pacific crestfish, lives in tropical and subtropical waters of the Pacific and Atlantic oceans. As larva, it measures no more than about 3 ⅛ inches long (8 cm). As an adult, reaching 2 ¼ to 3 ¼ feet (70 cm–1 m) with large individuals growing up to 6 ½ feet (2 m), it takes up residence in deeper waters. Swimming with its head held high, it has a sac of ink under the air bladder and a habit of ejecting black ink from the anus, presumably when it's frightened.

Amphipod on Rhizarians

Phronimopsis spinifera and Genus *Aulosphaera*
(Subclass Phaeodaria), species unknown

Here, tiny ⅛ inch (0.3 cm) mature hyperiid amphipods are shown floating with rhizarians, an abundant group of one-celled organisms that includes the foraminifera, radiolarians and these phaeodarians, in a newly described symbiosis discovered in Suruga Bay, Japan. By getting a lift with the rhizarians, the amphipods can obtain buoyancy and save swimming energy. Announcing the discovery in 2019, photographer Ryo Minemizu and colleagues published a paper in *Marine Biodiversity* referring to the amphipods as "rhizarian riders."

Peppermint Shrimp
Genus *Lysmata*, species unknown

This young peppermint shrimp, in the zoeal larva stage, measures just ⅝ inch long (1.5 cm). Peppermint shrimp larvae are known for their flamboyant colors, but this one, with its unique paddles (to help it keep balance? to attract prey? to distract predators?), takes the prize.

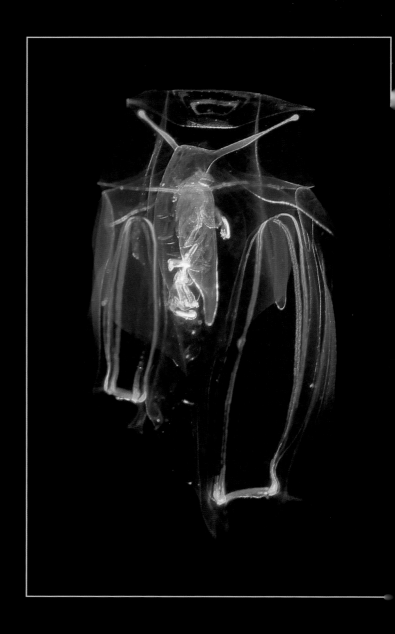

Siphonophore

Ceratocymba leuckartii

This ¾ inch (2 cm) mature siphonophore is entering the eudoxid, or sexual generation, stage. Shining fluorescent green, the gelatinous outer shell has the consistency of gummy candy.

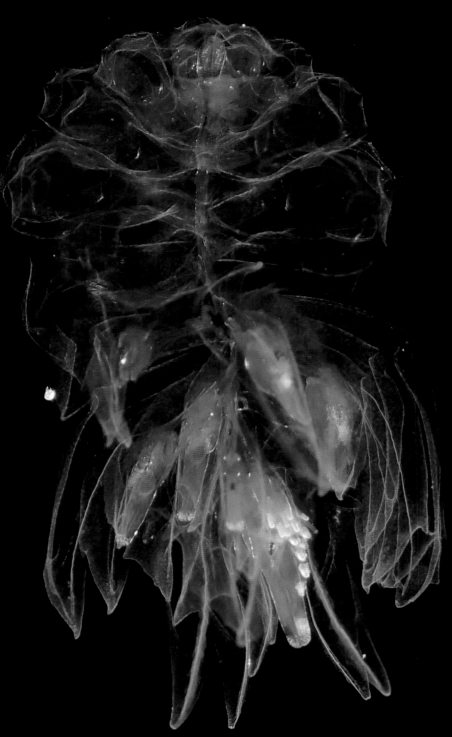

Jellyfish

Forskalia tholoides,
possible species identification

This juvenile siphonophore is only
⅝ inch long (1.5 cm). It was photographed in the waters around Osezaki in
Suruga Bay, Japan, in December. Some
siphonophores emit light to attract and
attack prey but, for unknown reasons,
this species glows fluorescent green
only in the juvenile stage. The red part
is a pneumatophore, or gas-filled float,
which helps them maintain buoyancy
at their preferred depth in the upper
waters near the surface.

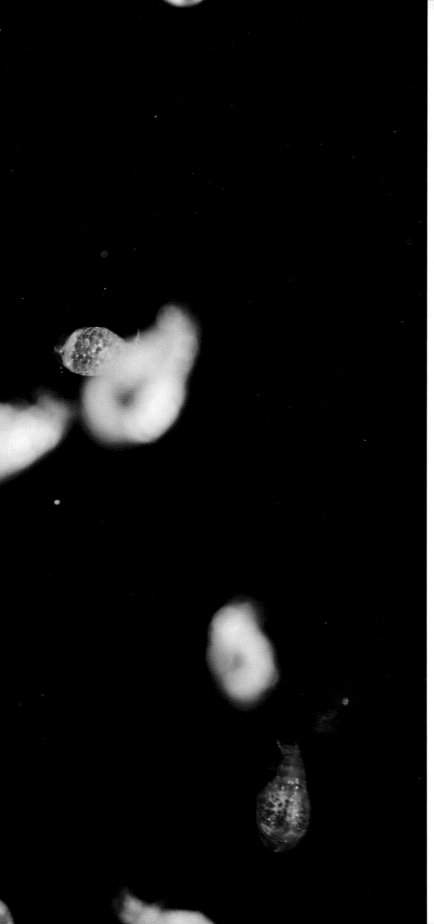

CHAPTER 7
Blackwater Unlimited

Photographs are being taken every night around the global ocean by blackwater divers who never know what will appear. So much of the ocean is unstudied and there are hundreds of thousands of species still unknown, unnamed, never even seen. Early mariners believed the ocean was filled with hungry creatures of the deep rising up from the depths to grab anything and everything. They got the size wrong, but otherwise they were right.

In this and the following chapter, we feature glimpses of plankton and other night creatures living in the waters of Green Island and Longdong, Taiwan; Kimbe Bay, Papua New Guinea; Palau; Raja Ampat, Lembeh and Ambon in Indonesia; the Sea of Japan/East Sea off Russia; and off Ponza Island, Italy, and other locations in the Mediterranean.

« Salp with male Argonaut and Hyperiid residents

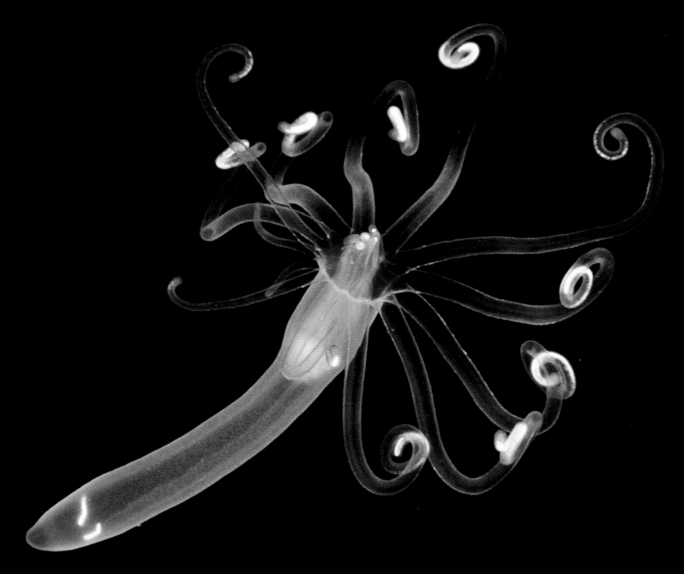

Tube Anemone

Subclass Cerantharia, species unknown

This larval cerantharian, or tube-dwelling anemone, was found in the waters of Ambon, Indonesia. Measuring only ½ inch (1.3 cm), it will eventually settle in the sediment, partly burying itself for protection. For now, it enjoys the night life, catching small plankton and nutrients in the upper waters.

Left-handed Hermit Crab

Family Diogenidae, species unknown

Left-handed hermit crabs belong to a family that, as adults, all have the left claw, or chela, larger than the right, as opposed to the more typical right-handed hermit crabs. There are more than 400 species of left-handed hermits. This ½ inch (1.3 cm) individual from Lembeh, Indonesia, is in the megalopa larval form, in which the crab is still swimming in the transitional phase after being a planktonic zoea and before it settles on the bottom as an adult crab and starts the quest to find an abandoned shell to serve as a protective home. Some hermit crabs live up to 10 years, others much longer.

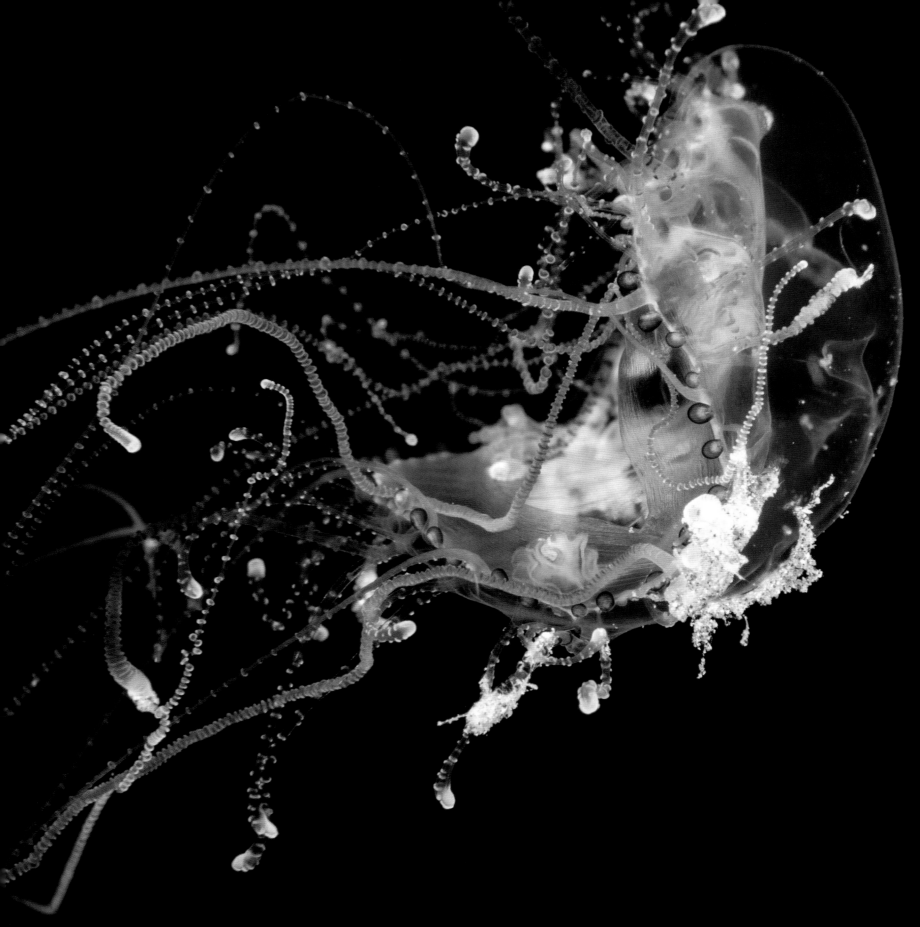

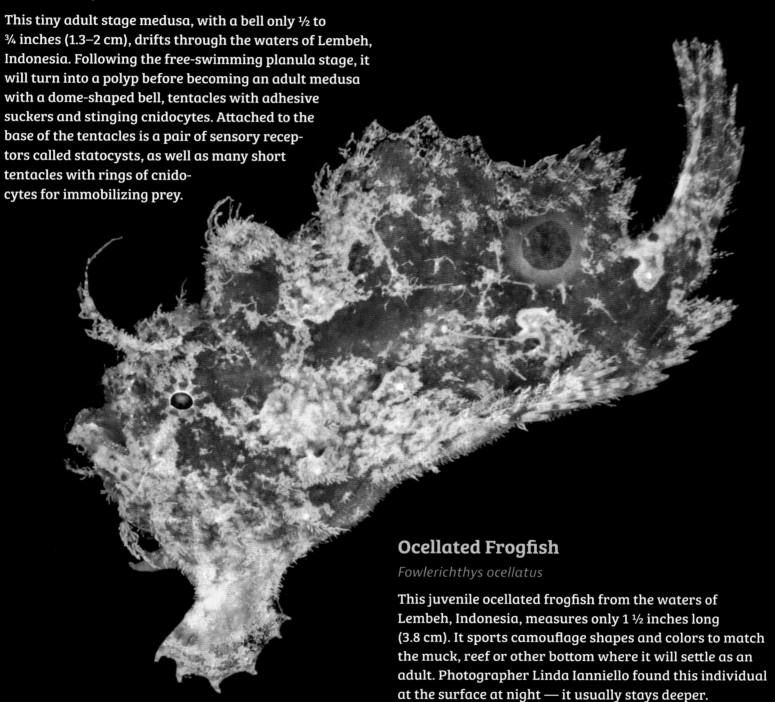

Hydromedusa (left)

Olindias malayensis

This tiny adult stage medusa, with a bell only ½ to ¾ inches (1.3–2 cm), drifts through the waters of Lembeh, Indonesia. Following the free-swimming planula stage, it will turn into a polyp before becoming an adult medusa with a dome-shaped bell, tentacles with adhesive suckers and stinging cnidocytes. Attached to the base of the tentacles is a pair of sensory receptors called statocysts, as well as many short tentacles with rings of cnidocytes for immobilizing prey.

Ocellated Frogfish

Fowlerichthys ocellatus

This juvenile ocellated frogfish from the waters of Lembeh, Indonesia, measures only 1 ½ inches long (3.8 cm). It sports camouflage shapes and colors to match the muck, reef or other bottom where it will settle as an adult. Photographer Linda Ianniello found this individual at the surface at night — it usually stays deeper.

147

Slipper Lobster riding a Hydromedusa

Family Scyllaridae and Hydromedusa species, both unknown

Slipper lobsters in the phyllosoma or larval stage love to ride on single gelatinous zooplankton ranging from comb jellies, jellyfish, sea jellies, salps and arrow worms. "Phyllosoma" is the term used for larval spiny, slipper and coral lobsters, all of which belong to the Achelata (claw-less) group of lobsters. They are difficult to identify to the species in this larval stage. These phyllosomae all have thin, flat, transparent bodies with long legs. During a year in the life, there are 10 phyllosoma stages from egg to adult in which individuals may range in size from 0.05 to 2 inches (0.13 to 5 cm). As adults, slipper lobsters can measure 2 to 20 inches (5–50 cm), depending on the species. They settle on the bottom and are found at depths of up to 1,640 feet (500 m).

Shrimp

Order Decapoda, species unknown

This presumed larval shrimp, resident to Lembeh, Indonesia, measures ¾ inch long (2 cm), not including the eyes which are perched at the end of long stalks. Little is known about larval shrimp. Marine biologists of the future have an open field if they want to classify and study the developmental biology and behavior of shrimp.

Polychaete Worm
Family Syllidae, species unknown

This planktonic polychaete worm measures only a little more than ¼ inch long (0.7 cm). It moves nimbly, ranging from shallow to deep water, often living in bottom sediment but popping up to breed. This one was photographed in the Sea of Japan, also known as the East Sea, off southeastern Russia.

Salp with male Argonaut and Hyperiids (right)
Family Salpidae, Genus *Argonauta* and Order Amphipoda, species unknown

A window on the blackwater Mediterranean off Italy: A male argonaut, or paper nautilus, about ⁵⁄₁₆ inch long (0.8 cm), perches on part of a salp colony, surrounded by hyperiids, tiny big-eyed marine amphipods. Some paper nautili will actually burrow inside a salp, perhaps to avoid predation while having access to a ready food supply.

Isopod riding on plastic wrapping (left)

Order Isopoda, species unknown

Isopods are an order of marine crustaceans related to the terrestrial pill bugs or woodlice. At night in the Mediterranean Sea, many of them can be found in surface waters and they are often found riding bits of garbage or bird feathers and will even settle on the camera housings of blackwater photographers. This one is less than ⅜ inch long (0.7–1 cm) and has landed on a cigarette pack wrapping.

Bobtail Squid mating

Sepiola atlantica, probable identification

Off Ponza Island in the Mediterranean Sea, at a depth of 23 to 40 feet (7–12 m), biologist-photographer Alexander Semenov found these two bobtail squid mating at night in April 2020. The giant eyes of both squid are peeled for predators or rivals who might disturb them. Length of each squid is ¾ inch (2 cm).

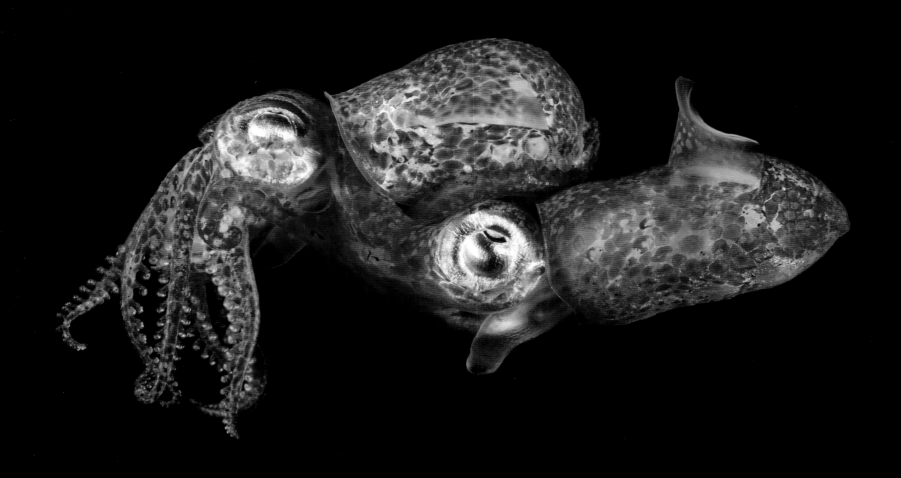

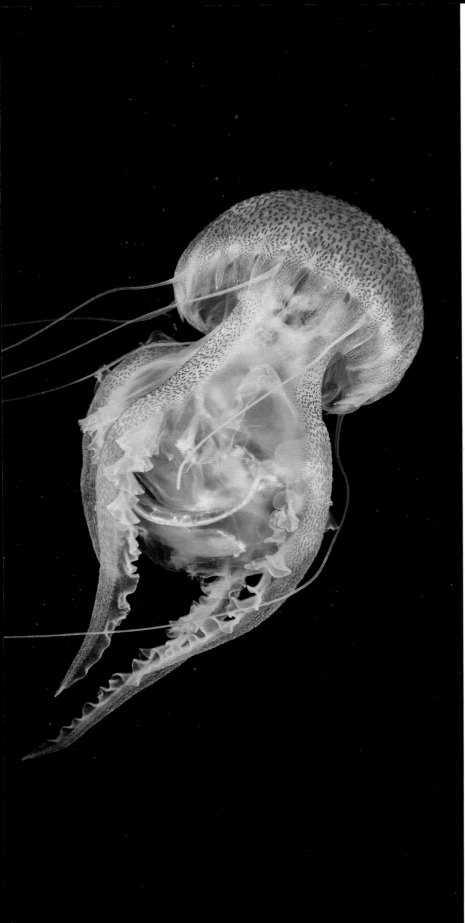

CHAPTER 8

From Blackwater Passion to Protection

Several of the blackwater diving sites in this book are inside marine protected areas (MPAs) such as in the Philippines, around Anilao, and in the White Sea of Russia. Still to be protected are the sites off Kona, Hawai'i; southeast Florida in the Gulf Stream; and Suruga Bay and Kure Island, Japan. The Kona Coast of Hawai'i Important Marine Mammal Area (IMMA) was identified for spinner dolphins who typically come in every morning to rest close to shore after a long night of hunting in the blackwater. Much of the Kona Coast is also within the West Hawai'i Regional Fisheries Management Area, which places some restrictions on fishing. This helps signal the importance of this area, but the recognition doesn't extend offshore to prime blackwater spots. And the southeast Florida site at the edge of the Gulf Stream is located a couple hundred miles from the recently proposed Sargasso Sea High Seas Marine Protected Area, which the Convention on Biological Diversity has also identified as an ecologically or biologically significant area. However, in all five locations, even where there is a measure of protection, the bottom fauna and the entire water column, as well as the ecosystem supporting the vertical migration of plankton, are not protected in a comprehensive way.

Across the vastness of the ocean, less than 8% of the surface area is protected, but the protection often does not cover the seabed and the water column. In the high seas, where more than half of the world ocean is located, just 1% of the surface area is protected.

« **Mauve stinger capturing a salp**

Another pressing problem for the health of the ocean, the result of surging nutrient inputs from human activities on land and subject to increase in the future from climate change, is the loss of life-sustaining oxygen in the sea's middle to bottom layers. This oxygen loss, or deoxygenation, is creating more and more oxygen-minimum zones in the ocean. In some parts of the ocean, zooplankton are dying from lack of oxygen and others are thought to be near the limit of their ability to survive. At the same time, parts of the ocean, due to climate change, are becoming more and more acidic. Jellyfish don't mind acidic conditions and some seem to thrive while most zooplankton and other species die out or are displaced. This particularly affects species such as sea butterflies (pteropods) that have calcium carbonate shells. It may also affect skeletal development in larval fishes.

The vertical migration of plankton is a common feature of the world ocean, and absolutely essential as it forges the link between primary producers, the phytoplankton, and the big predators including fish, squid, whales and dolphins. The feeding, defecation, respiration of all these species in the water column are responsible for the vertical transport of carbon and particles to the depths as part of the biological pump that also serves as a safety valve for excess carbon in the atmosphere. Without healthy plankton, the food base in the ocean would be disrupted, placing populations of larger animals at risk.

Many of the vertical migrators are extraordinary species, living in ecosystems that scientists are only beginning to study, such as are shown in these pages in the Mediterranean, Palau, Taiwan and Indonesia. We need more research and broader ecosystem management of the ocean. We need large, strictly protected marine areas. We need to be able to confront the challenges around pollution, deoxygenation and climate change including acidification, sea-level rise and the potential slowing or other disturbance of ocean currents. Ultimately, successful ecosystem management comes down to protection measures for the planet and the requirement that humans stop polluting and contributing to global warming. Legal measures and enforcement can change the way industry behaves, but achieving success requires all of us to change the way we think, what we care about, and how we act. If humans can learn to care for the ocean, this will offer the best chance to maintain natural systems, including the wondrous phenomenon of the vertical migration of plankton.

The extraordinary biological diversity of the species that we celebrate in this book is presented in hope that we can all be inspired to help maintain healthy seas.

Planktonic love — that's what we need.

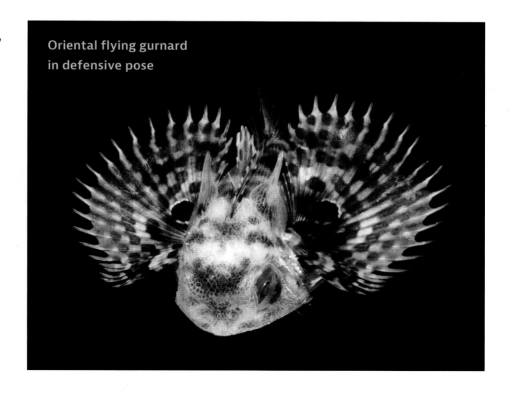

Oriental flying gurnard in defensive pose

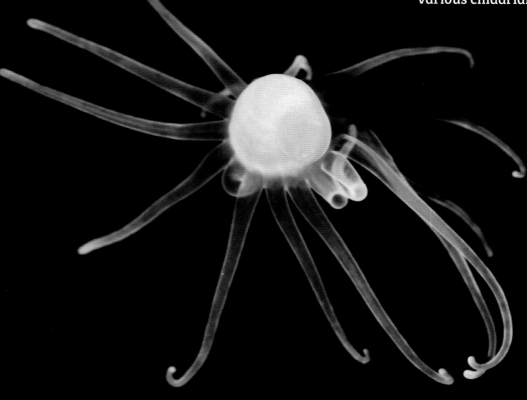

Jack and Anemone

Family Carangidae and Phylum Cnidaria,
both species unknown

Photographed in Kimbe Bay, Papua New Guinea, this juvenile jack, 2 inches long (5 cm), likes to hang out with various cnidarians, in this case with a larval anemone.

Mauve Stinger capturing a Salp (left)

Pelagia noctiluca and Subphylum Tunicata,
species unknown

A common jellyfish in the Mediterranean Sea, the mauve stinger has stinging cells not only on the arms but on the dome as well. Here, a 4 ¾ to 8 inch (12–20 cm) individual has captured a salp and is feeding on it. Hunting both day and night, mauve stingers form huge jellyfish blooms in some areas. The mauve stinger can glow bright blue when it's disturbed.

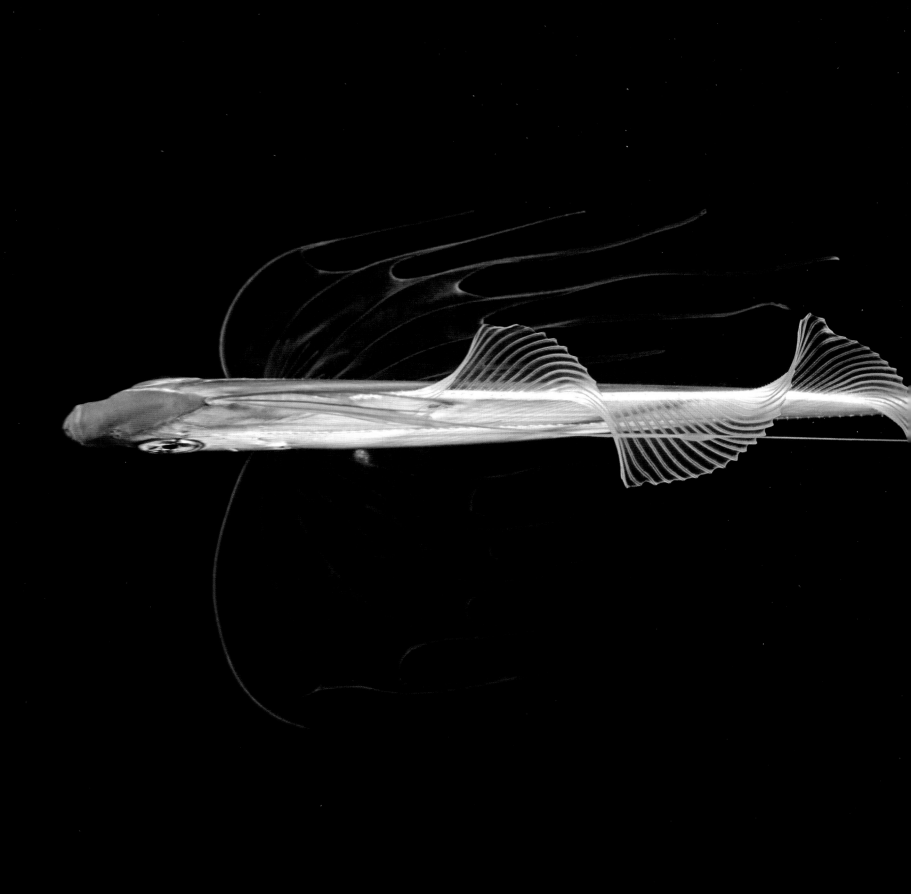

Mediterranean Dealfish

Trachipterus trachypterus

This flashy streamlined larval individual, measuring
5 to 8 inches long (12–20 cm), inhabits the waters of the
western Mediterranean around Italy. The long, filamentous pelvic fins resemble jellyfish tentacles, and the
extended caudal-fin rays mimic a jellyfish dome, poten-
tially deterring predators. Every night, they swim up to
surface waters to hunt, catching small worms, larval
shrimp and squid.

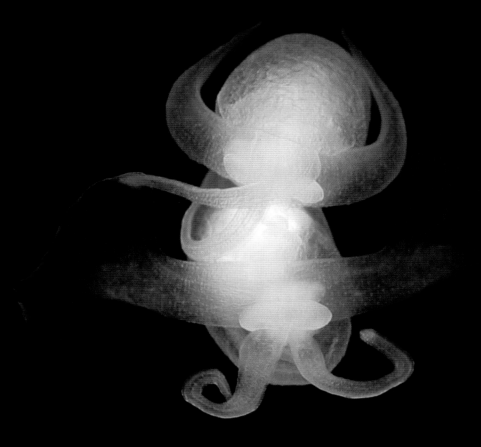

Sea Angel

Hydromyles globulosus

A sea angel, ⁵⁄₁₆ inch (0.8 cm), flutters its wings, in search of a mate. It could be male or female. In fact, sea angels start out as males, developing eggs as they mature. Thus, adults have both spermatozoa and eggs in their bodies and can go either way when they encounter a mate. Sea angels are marine slugs with an endearing appearance and swimming style. They are also fierce and voracious predators, preying on sea butterflies.

Oriental Flying Gurnard (right)

Dactyloptena orientalis

In the waters of Palau, a larval oriental flying gurnard spreads its full 1 ⁹⁄₁₆ inch (4 cm) frame into a defensive posture. The body is protected by sharp spines extending from the head. There is a black eye spot on the huge round pectoral fin. The name "gurnard" comes from the French, meaning to grunt, because of the grunting sound this fish makes. Once mature, it will have a heavily armored, sturdy body reaching up to 16 inches long (40 cm) but more commonly 8 inches (20 cm). The mature oriental flying gurnard will often glide just above the bottom, where the fish is camouflaged. If threatened, however, it will spread its huge pectoral fins to make itself look larger.

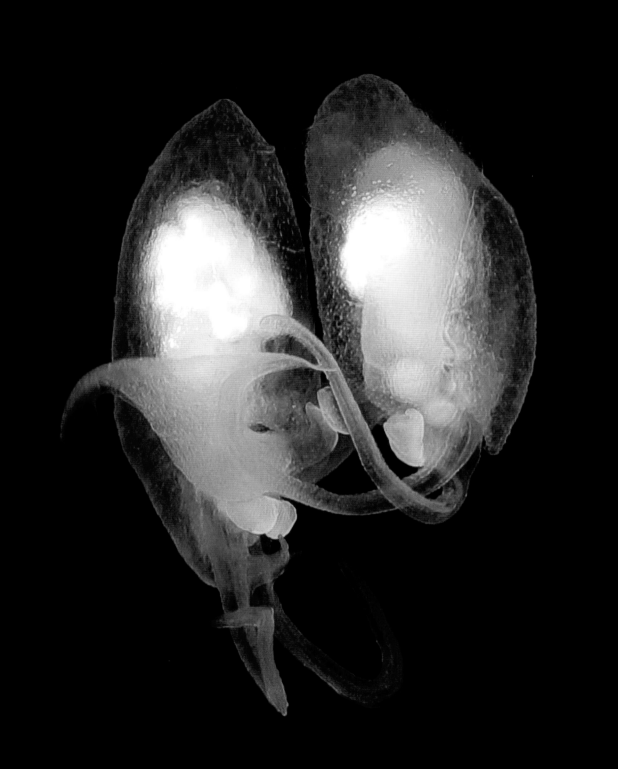

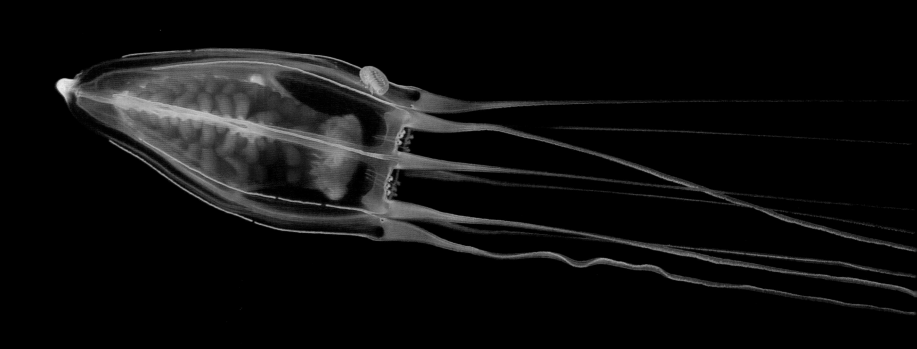

Sea Angels (left)

Hydromyles globulosus

Sea angels meet in the waters of Palau in the tropical western Pacific. These mature sea angels, each presenting as both male and female, are only 5/16 inch long (0.8 cm). When they meet, they swim alongside each other in what has been described as a mating dance. They then turn out their reproductive organs, attaching themselves to the other with a sucker. After four hours, the time needed for fertilization, the sucker leaves a scar on both individuals as a souvenir of having mated. To disconnect, they start spinning. Mature sea angels carry up to four scars matching the number of mating rituals they have gone through. Even during the mating process the sea angels continue their graceful swim and they will hunt together to satisfy their appetite.

Jellyfish and Amphipod

Family Pandeidae, probably *Eutiara decorata*, and Family Hyperiidae, species unknown

This 1 1/8 inch (2.8 cm) nearly mature jellyfish is transparent, with its red gonad, or reproductive gland, clearly showing. The amphipod may be parasitic on jellyfish but also eager for a free ride.

Bigfin Reef Squid
Sepioteuthis lessoniana

The nighttime hunter pauses for a moment. This mature bigfin reef squid, 6 inches long (15 cm), hovers in open water above the coral reef in Dampier Strait, Raja Ampat in West Papua, Indonesia. This species is found only in the tropical Indo-Pacific region.

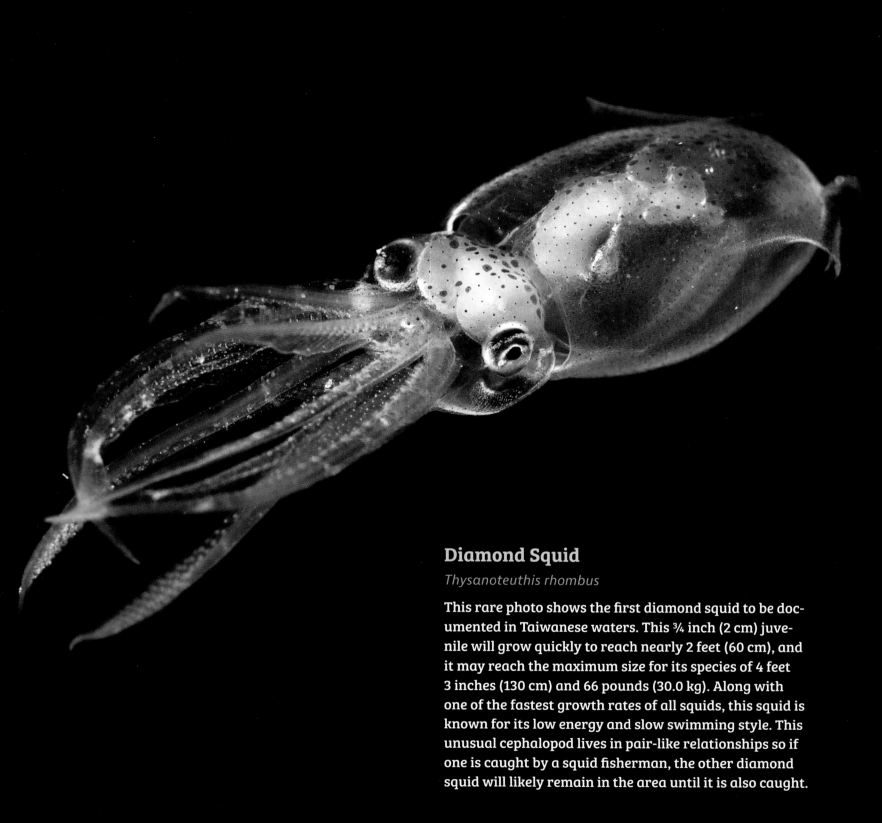

Diamond Squid

Thysanoteuthis rhombus

This rare photo shows the first diamond squid to be documented in Taiwanese waters. This ¾ inch (2 cm) juvenile will grow quickly to reach nearly 2 feet (60 cm), and it may reach the maximum size for its species of 4 feet 3 inches (130 cm) and 66 pounds (30.0 kg). Along with one of the fastest growth rates of all squids, this squid is known for its low energy and slow swimming style. This unusual cephalopod lives in pair-like relationships so if one is caught by a squid fisherman, the other diamond squid will likely remain in the area until it is also caught.

Bigfin Reef Squid

Sepioteuthis lessoniana

At night, the bigfin reef squid prowl the waters off Longdong, northeastern Taiwan, one of the most abundant marine life areas in this part of the world.

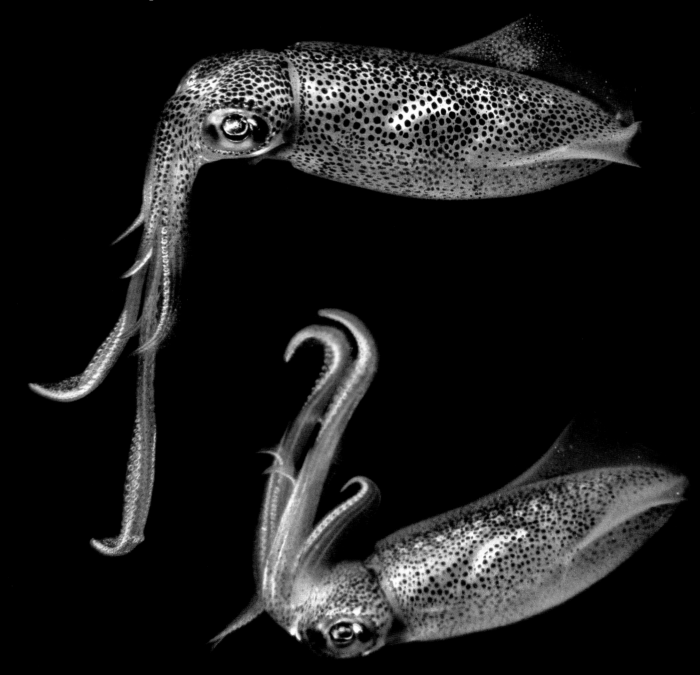

Black-blotched Porcupinefish

Diodon liturosus

A fresh-faced juvenile porcupinefish pokes its head into the upper waters around Green Island, off Taiwan, at night. This fish is usually solitary, staying quiet and hidden during most daylight hours. It maintains an active night life even as it grows into adulthood. It grows up to 25 ½ inches long (65 cm). This porcupinefish seems to have a smirk on its face. Even though it is a poor swimmer, if danger arises, the fish inflates itself by swallowing water until it is completely round and all its spines point straight out. Its skin contains a toxin called tetrodotoxin, which is at least 1,200 times more toxic than cyanide. The toxin is produced by bacteria from the fish's diet. In *The Voyage of the Beagle*, Charles Darwin related a secondhand story of a porcupinefish that had been swallowed by a large shark and then had eaten its way out through the body. A good story but unlikely to be true. However, porcupinefish have been documented to kill sharks by inflating part-way down the gullet, causing the shark to asphyxiate but killing the porcupinefish, too.

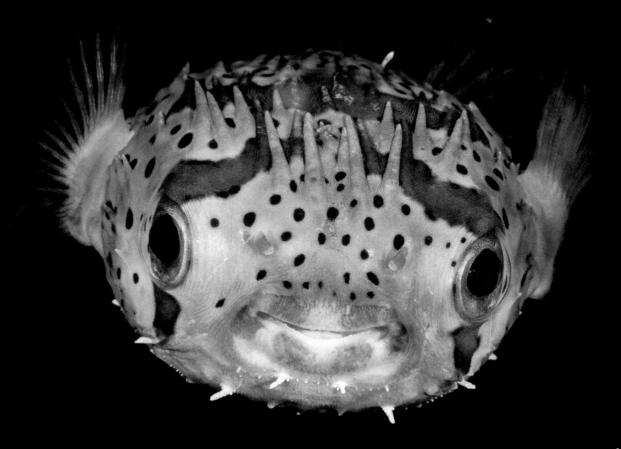

Sources

Frazer, J. (2014). How zooplankton bust a move. *Scientific American* [Blog]. https://blogs.scientificamerican.com/artful-amoeba/how-zooplankton-bust-a-move/

Froese, R. & Pauly, D. Editors. (2022). FishBase. Also: Horton, T. et al. (2022). World Amphipoda Database. Madin, L. (2022). World List of Thaliacea. MolluscaBase eds. (2022). MolluscaBase. Molodtsova, T. (2022). World List of Ceriantharia. Read, G. & Fauchald, K. (Ed.) (2022). World Polychaeta Database. Saiz, J. (2022). World Sipuncula Database. Schuchert, P. (2022). World Hydrozoa Database. WoRMS (2022). All Accessed through: World Register of Marine Species at: https://www.marinespecies.org.

Hamner, W. M. (1975). Underwater observations of blue-water plankton: Logistics, techniques, and safety procedures for divers at sea. *Limnology and Oceanography, 20*(6), 1045–1051.

Hoyt, E. (2020). *Strange sea creatures.* Firefly Books.

Hoyt, E. (2021). *Creatures of the deep* [Updated 3rd ed.]. Firefly Books.

Ianniello, L., & Mears, S. (2021). *Blackwater creatures. A guide to Southeast Florida blackwater diving.* [2nd ed.].

Kirby, R.R. (2010). *Ocean drifters: A secret world beneath the waves.* Firefly Books.

Kiørboe T., Jiang, H., Gonçalves, R. J., Nielsen, L. T., & Wadhwa, N. (2014). Flow disturbances generated by feeding and swimming zooplankton. *Proceedings of the National Academy of Sciences, 111*(32),11738–11743. https://doi.org/10.1073/pnas.1405260111

McGreevy, N. (2020, April 10). Watch this giant, eerie, string-like sea creature hunt for food in the Indian Ocean. *Smithsonian Magazine.*

Milisen, J. (2020). *A field guide to blackwater diving in Hawai'i.* Mutual Publishing.

Milisen, J. W., Matye, S. A., & Kobayashi, D. R. (2018). Nocturnal visual census of pelagic fauna using scuba near Kona, Hawai'i. *Pacific Science, 72*(4), 399–410.

Nakamura, Y., Minemizu, R., & Saito, N. (2019). "Rhizarian rider"—symbiosis between *Phronimopsis spinifera* Claus, 1879 (Amphipoda) and *Aulosphaera* sp. (Phaeodaria). *Marine Biodiversity, 49*(5), 2193–2195.

Newbert, C. (1982) *Within a rainbowed sea.* Beyond Words Publishing.

Nonaka, A., Milisen, J. W., Mundy, B. C., & Johnson, G. D. (2021). Blackwater diving: An exciting window into the planktonic arena and its potential to enhance the quality of larval fish collections. *Ichthyology & Herpetology, 109*(1):138–156. https://doi.org/10.1643/i2019318

Olsen, E. (2021, March 30) The ocean's youngest monsters are ready for glamour shots. *The New York Times.* Retrieved August 06, 2021, from https://www.nytimes.com/2021/03/30/science/blackwater-photography-fish-larvae.html

Robertson-Brown, N., & Robertson-Brown, C. (2020, August 3). Diving with... Mike Bartick, Crystal Blue Resort, Anilao, Philippines. Scubaverse. https://www.scubaverse.com/diving-with-mike-bartick-crystal-blue-resort-anilao-philippines/

Schuchert, P. & Collins, R. (2021). Hydromedusae observed during night dives in the Gulf Stream. *Revue Suisse de Zoologie, 128*(2):237-356. https://doi.org/10.35929/RSZ.0049

Spiers, H. (2018, December 28). Conversation with Mike Bartick. Henley Spiers Photography. https://www.henleyspiers.com/blog/2018/12/31/conversation-with-mike-bartick

Wishner, K. F., Seibel, B. A., Roman, C., Deutsch, C., Outram, D., Shaw, C. T., Birk, M. A., Mislan, K. A. S., Adams, T. J., Moore, D., & Riley, S. (2018). Ocean deoxygenation and zooplankton: Very small oxygen differences matter. *Science Advances, 4*(12), eaau5180. https://doi.org/10.1126/sciadv.aau5180

Glossary

Actinia A kind of sea anemone in the order Actiniaria.

Amphipod A species in the order Amphipoda consisting of mainly marine crustaceans with no carapace and a laterally compressed body.

Annelid worm The large phylum, or group, of segmented worms including ragworms, earthworms and leeches.

Anthomedusa A member of the order Anthoathecata, also called Anthomedusae, which includes hydroid coelenterates having a polyp stage but lacking a perisarc and free-living medusa stage.

Appendicularians The larvaceans; see *larvaceans*.

Ascidians Species in the class Ascidiacea of solitary or colonial sessile tunicates having an incurrent and a siphon, also called a sea squirt.

Auricularia The first larval stage of a sea cucumber.

Bell The umbrella-shaped hood or dome which forms the main part of the body of a jellyfish from which tentacles are suspended.

Benthic Referring to organisms that live in the ecological region on the bottom of the sea.

Biological (Linnean) classification system All named organisms fit into various levels of taxa, presented here from general to the most specific: domain, kingdom, phylum, class, order, family, genus and species.

Bioluminescence The production and emission of light by a living organism, including vertebrates, invertebrates, fungi and bacteria.

Blackwater diving A night dive, usually in open water, using high-powered light sources, generally focused on finding planktonic creatures and other vertical migrators.

Bluewater diving A day-time dive in open water.

Cephalopod A member of the class Cephalopoda, including squid, octopus, cuttlefish and nautilus, typically active predatory mollusks.

Cerata Protrusions on the body of a nudibranch.

Ceriantharia Subclass of tube-dwelling anemones.

Chromatophore Cell or group of cells containing pigments which reflect light.

Cilia Short, hairlike protrusions growing from cells; can be used by zooplankton for propulsion or to disturb the water.

Cirri Flexible tendrils.

Cnidarian Any invertebrate marine animal (jellyfish, sea anemone, coral) belonging to the phylum Cnidaria characterized by stinging structures in the tentacles surrounding the mouth.

Comb jelly Marine invertebrate of the phylum of ctenophores with a gelatinous nearly transparent body, usually bioluminescent and propelling itself with rows of fused cilia.

Crustacean An animal in the large class of mainly aquatic arthropods with mandibles and a chitinous exoskeleton. Crustaceans include crabs, shrimp, mantis shrimp, lobsters, squat lobsters, amphipods, copepods and barnacles.

Ctenophore See *comb jelly*.

Decapod Crustacean of the order Decapoda including shrimp, prawn, crab and lobster.

Dinoflagellate One-celled aquatic organism that swims using two dissimilar flagellae and comprises a major part of the phytoplankton, a link in the food chain and a common bioluminescent organism.

Doliolaria One of the middle larval stages of a sea cucumber.

Dorsal fin The fin on the back of most fish, whales and dolphins and other aquatic vertebrates.

Echinoderm A marine invertebrate of the phylum Echinodermata, such as a starfish, sea urchin or sea cucumber. Adults have radial symmetry.

Ephyra Free-swimming larval stage of jellyfish development.

Eudoxid The sexual generation stage of a mature siphonophore.

Euphausiid Krill.

Euston Free-swimming larval stage of jellyfish development.

Foraminiferan A single-celled organism, member of the phylum Foraminifera. A one-celled protist.

Gastropod A mollusk such as a slug or snail, sometimes with a shell and a distinct head carrying sensory organs.

Gelatinous zooplankton An informal group that includes jellyfish, salps, siphonophores, pyrozomes, comb jellies and other ctenophores.

Hemichordate A marine invertebrate of the phylum Hemichordata of wormlike marine animals, such as an acorn worm.

Heteropod A species in a group of pelagic gastropods (mollusks).

Hydroid A life stage for animals related to jellyfish in the class Hydrozoa. Most hydroids are colonial with individual polyps specialized for feeding and reproduction while others are solitary.

Hydromedusa The medusa form of a hydrozoan produced asexually by budding from a hydroid.

Hydrozoan A species in the class of small, predatory, mostly marine animals, some solitary and some living in groups. The colonies of these species can be large and, in some cases, the specialized individual animals cannot survive outside the colony. Hydrozoans are related to jellyfish and corals and are sometimes referred to as jellyfish.

Hyperiid Any of a number of species of small marine crustaceans called amphipods; a member of the suborder Hyperiidea.

Isopod Member of the large order of aquatic crustaceans (Isopoda) with the body composed of seven free thoracic segments each with a pair of matching legs; related to terrestrial pill bugs.

Larvacean Any of the species of solitary, free-swimming, filter-feeding tunicates that live in the open ocean; they are members of the class Appendicularia.

Mantle The umbrella-shaped top of most cnidarians including jellyfish, also sometimes referred to as the bell; also used to describe the sheath of muscle around the body, behind the head, of cephalopods.

Maxillipeds The appendages in crustaceans modified for feeding positioned in pairs behind the maxillae or mouthparts.

Medusa One of the two main body types of cnidarians besides polyps. The medusa form is shaped like a bell or umbrella.

Metamorphosis The process of transformation from immature to adult form in two or more stages.

Micronekton The tiny animals that can actively swim against the ocean currents.

Mollusks A large phylum of animals that are invertebrates with a soft unsegmented body, many with a calcium carbonate shell, including squid, octopus, sea butterflies, sea angels, pelagic nudibranchs and marine snail veligers.

Nekton Aquatic animals that can swim and move independently of water currents.

Nematocyst The stinging cell in the tentacles of cnidarians such as jellyfish. A nematocyst is a capsule containing a barbed tube that produces a sting that can be toxic to predators and prey.

Neuston The habitat at the interface between the sea surface and the atmosphere or immediately below it. Also the organisms that live in that habitat.

Nudibranch A shell-less, soft-bodied marine snail or gastropod with appendages on the back and sides used for respiration.

Octopod Any of the eight-armed animals in the order Octopoda of cephalopod mollusks, including argonaut and octopus species.

Ossicles Tiny pieces of calcified material that creates small protrusions from the body wall of a sea cucumber.

Paralarvae Young cephalopods in the planktonic stages between hatching and becoming a subadult.

Pectoral fin The pair of side fins, sometimes called breast fins or flippers.

Pelagic Living in the water column and not on the bottom of the sea.

Pelagosphaera The secondary free-swimming larvae of the Sipuncula (unsegmented) marine worms.

Pentacula One of the later larval stages of the sea cucumber.

Pereopods The eight appendages of crabs or lobsters growing from the thorax and used for locomotion.

Photophore The luminous spot on various fishes and cephalopods; a glandular organ specialized to produce light; see *bioluminescence*.

Phyllosoma The larval stage of spiny, slipper and coral lobsters.

Phytoplankton Plant plankton; see *plankton*.

Plankton Organisms that drift in the ocean currents, contrasted to those that swim. A primary food for many animals, plankton includes both phytoplankton — plant-based organisms including microscopic algae — and zooplankton — animal organisms such as copepods and many larval stages of fishes and invertebrates. (Plankter is the singular term.)

Pleopods Paired-like appendages that shrimp use for swimming and carrying eggs.

Pneumatophore Gas-filled float which helps siphonophores float on the surface.

Polychaete An annelid worm, characterized by a segmented body; bristle worm.

Polyp The hollow, columnar, sessile (attached) form of cnidarians (as opposed to the medusa form).

Pteropod Sea butterfly, free-swimming marine sea snail or sea slug.

Pyrosome A free floating genus of colonial tunicates made up of hundreds to thousands of individuals called zooids.

Rhizarian An organism in the species-rich supergroup comprised of mainly single cell organisms.

Salp A marine invertebrate, a tunicate, with a transparent barrel-shaped body.

Sargassum Refers to the brown algae of many species found around the world, but famously growing in great abundance in the Sargasso Sea.

Sea sapphire A kind of copepod.

Symbiotic Interaction between two different organisms that live in close physical association. The symbiosis may benefit only one organism or be mutually beneficial.

Scyphozoa The marine class of the phylum Cnidaria comprising true jellyfish.

Siphonophore One of the swimming or floating colonies of marine hydrozoans in the order Siphonophora, such as the Portuguese man o' war.

Stomatopod A species in the mantis shrimp group consisting of more than 400 species.

Tentillae The branches of a tentacle, such as on a squid.

Tornaria The larval stage of the acorn worm.

Tunicate A marine invertebrate member of the subphylum Tunicata. It is part of the Chordata, a phylum which includes all animals with dorsal nerve cords and notochords. Their name derives from their unique outer covering or "tunic," which is formed from proteins and carbohydrates, and acts as an exoskeleton.

Veliger The final larval stage of certain mollusks.

Ventral On the underside of an animal.

Vertical migration Also called diel or diurnal vertical migration, it is a pattern of movement used by plankton and other organisms to feed mainly at night in the upper waters of the ocean.

Zoea The free-swimming larvae of decapod crustaceans such as crabs and lobsters.

Zooid A single animal arising from another by budding to form a colony.

Zooplankton Animal plankton; see *plankton*.

Photography Credits

Photographs © Alex Mustard/Nature Public Library, 8, 12–13, 164

Photographs © Alexander Semenov, 6–7, 10, 106, 107, 108, 108 (inset), 109, 110, 111, 112–113, 114, 115, 116, 117, 118, 119, 142–143, 150, 151, 152, 153, 154, 156, 158–159

Photographs © David Hall/Nature Public Library, 2, 16–17

Photographs © Doug Perrine/Nature Public Library, 21, 38, 39, 40, 41

Photographs © Jeff Milisen, 18, 19, 20, 22, 23, 24–25, 26, 27, 28–29, 30, 31, 32, 33, 34, 35, 36, 37, 157

Photographs © Linda Ianniello, 78, 79, 80, 81, 82, 83, 84, 85, 86, 87, 88, 89, 90, 91, 92, 93, 94, 95, 96, 97, 98, 98 (inset), 99, 100, 101, 144, 145, 146, 147, 148

Photographs © Mike Bartick, 63, 64, 65, 66, 67, 68, 69, 70, 71, 72, 72 (inset), 73, 74, 75, 76, 105

Photographs © Magnus Lundgren/Nature Public Library, 43, 44, 45, 50, 51, 52–53, 54, 55, 56, 57, 58, 59, 60, 61, 62, 77, 165, 166, 167, 176, 177

Photographs © Pascal Kobeh/Nature Public Library, 14–15

Photographs © Ryo Minemizu 42, 46, 47, 48–49, 120, 121, 122, 122 (inset), 123, 124, 125, 126, 127, 128, 129, 130, 131, 132, 133, 134, 135, 136, 137, 138, 139, 140, 140 (inset), 141, 155, 160, 161, 162, 163

Photographs © Susan Mears, 102, 103, 104, 149, 172

« Larval soapfish swimming at the edge of the Gulf Stream

Index

Larval anemone floating
in Balayan Bay, Anilao